COLLEGE ADMISSIONS MADE EASY:

A STEP-BY-STEP GUIDE

BY

GLENDA DURANO

Copyright © Glenda Durano 2021

Table of Contents

Introduction 1

How to Use This Book 2

Chapter 1: An Overview 3
    Seven Steps for Success 3
    The Pandemic Pivot 5
    A College Planning Timeline: One Year at a Time 6

Chapter 2: You-niversity Utopia Part One 13
    Start with the Student 13

Chapter 3: What Do You Want to Be When You Grow Up? 20
    Choosing a Major Using Assessments 20
    Shadowing 22

Chapter 4: You-niversity Utopia Part Two 24
    It's All About the Match 24
    Developing Your List 26
    Refining Your List 28
    Creating Questions 30

Chapter 5: Getting to Know You 33
    Prospective Student Experiences 34
    Virtual Visits 34
    The Phone Call 35
    Planning the Visit 38
    On Campus 40
    What If I Can't Visit? 41

Chapter 6: Show Me the Money 44
    Scholarships and Financial Aid 46
    Need-Based Money: FAFSA and the EFC 47
    Loans 50
    Other Forms of Need-Based Aid 51
    Additional Issues in Need-Based Aid 51
    Merit-Based Money 53
    Outside Scholarships 54
    Other Financial Considerations 58

Chapter 7: This is a Test 62
Test Types and Explanations 63
ACT versus SAT 65
Test Success 68

Chapter 8: Special Circumstances 71
Arts Programs 71
Honors College 72
Direct-entry Majors 72
Athletic Recruiting 73
GED 73
Homeschool Notes 73

Chapter 9: Applying to College 76
Overview 76
Getting a Jump on Applications 80
The Resumé: Who Are You? 81
The College Essay: Getting the Inside Out 83
Going Live 85
Recommendations 87
Requesting Transcripts and Scores 88
Staying on Time 89

Chapter 10: Decisions, Decisions... 90
Financial Appeals 90
Decision Time 91

Chapter 11: Is That All There Is? 93

A Request and a Special Offer 98

Appendix 99
Sample Resume 99
Sample College Visit Form 100
Sample Requirements Document 102
Sample Overall Timeline (partial) 104
Sample Homeschool Transcript 106
Sample Homeschool Course Descriptions 107

Endnotes 108

Introduction

The college admissions process can be overwhelming, BUT it doesn't have to be. This book is designed to help you cut through the craziness and get it done, simply and successfully.

The road to college has become riddled with insecurity and anxiety, causing untold frenzy among high school students. I want to repave that path with anticipation and excitement by answering the big and small questions that make the process so overwhelming, questions like:

- What's a good school?
- When should I begin my college search?
- How do I decide on a major?
- Are test scores important?
- What's a good essay topic?

I'll provide professional advice based on over a decade of college counseling experience and I'll break the process into manageable, attainable goals that result in an easy-to-follow, step-by-step roadmap for college admissions.

You won't find amusing stories about other people or statistics that make you want to cry because if you're like most college-bound students, you don't care about that right now. You're thinking, "Just tell me what to do."

So, that's what I'm going to do. Before you dive in, however, take a minute to read the section below called "How to Use This Book."

How to Use This Book

Reading this book all the way through will be overwhelming. Take it in bite-sized chunks. Start with the overview, evaluate where you are, determine whether you're on schedule, and decide how to proceed from there. You may need to catch up, fill in some holes, or find the answer to a burning question. This book will help you do all that and more.

The chapters are arranged sequentially, so you can certainly read through this book and navigate the process. Remember, however, college admissions is a deadline-driven process. Pay attention to the timeline. If you're already on track, you can use this book to answer your questions and fine tune your applications. Just turn to the chapter you need.

Whatever the case, let this book work for you. It's designed to make the college planning process less stressful and more successful.

One note: Throughout the book, I use the terms "college," "university," "school," and "institution" interchangeably. Please don't get distracted by the semantics.

Chapter 1

An Overview

College planning—preparing for any education after high school—is a journey with lots of twists and turns. While I know it's overwhelming to look at everything at once, getting a sense of the big picture will give you a good idea of what it will take for you to complete it.

People ask, "When should I start college planning?" In my opinion, the ideal time is the summer between the sophomore and junior years of high school. Many students, however, wait until later. If a student does wait until the end of his junior year or even the beginning of his senior year to start, it doesn't mean he won't succeed; it just means he needs to be diligent during the time he has left.

I don't recommend taking shortcuts. Every step is important, and when a student feels behind, it's tempting to skip certain steps. Please don't. This is your future, and you owe it to yourself to do the best you can.

Seven Steps for Success

Before I review the requirements in terms of an overall timeline, let me remind you of what I see as the "Seven Steps for Success" for the college-bound student.

1. Throughout high school, grades are important (even as a freshman). Do well. Take the most rigorous courses in which you can succeed. If your school offers higher level courses (Honors, AP, IB, Dual Credit), consider taking them. Colleges want students who are academically curious.

2. A student is more than his grades. Spend time outside the classroom being productive. This could mean taking part in sports, clubs, church activities, service, work, or family responsibilities. You don't have to participate in everything, but you should show commitment in more than one area of interest. Eventually, you should demonstrate leadership in at least one activity.
3. Many students discover their passions through volunteer work. Give back to the community—not simply out of obligation, but because you care.
4. Be productive during your summers. You could take on a seasonal, full-time job, develop skills through an internship, or serve others in a way that you don't have time to during the school year.
5. Apply for scholarships. Unfortunately, most students wait until it is too late to find outside scholarships to pay for education. Start early and be diligent. Apply for scholarships in your area of interest or expertise. Focus on those awards that require some work, not simply a sweepstakes. Students should apply for outside scholarships; however, most of your scholarship money will come from the institution you eventually attend. Colleges usually offer merit scholarships based on grades, scores, and extracurriculars. Be wise how you spend your time. See chapter six for details.
6. Believe it or not, your parents are on your side. They want nothing more than for you to succeed. Communicate with them and let them know you love and honor them.
7. Meet with your school guidance counselor regularly. It's your counselor's job to know what opportunities exist for students. Take advantage of that knowledge.

Note: Some families hire an independent education counselor to help them navigate the college planning process. An independent counselor can ultimately save a family time and money. Before you hire a counselor, make sure he is a member of the Higher Education Consultants Association (https://www.hecaonline.org/)

or the Independent Education Consultants Association (https://www.iecaonline.com/) and adheres to the NACAC code of ethics. Services vary but usually include helping the student create a college list (schools that are a good fit for the student academically, socially, and financially), preparing for standardized tests, editing essays, and overseeing the application process. You can find a local IEC by searching either of the two websites above.

The Pandemic Pivot

Before we continue, I need to address the massive changes to college admissions brought about by the 2020-21 pandemic. Coronavirus forced higher education to reinvent itself in many ways, and as a result, certain aspects of college admissions changed, notably:

- Standardized testing came to a grinding halt and, as a result, many universities stopped requiring a standardized test score as part of the college application.
- High schools transitioned to online classes: some for a few months and others for nearly a year. Because of this change, many high schools switched from giving letter grades to evaluating students with a pass/fail system. Colleges had to incorporate this modification in their evaluation of students' transcripts.
- On-campus college visits were cancelled. Virtual campus visits became the norm.
- Most extracurricular activities were cancelled. Consequently, online opportunities became more robust.
- With the economic downturn, college became less affordable for many families. Schools were forced to re-examine their scholarship and financial aid models.

These changes may seem scary, but here's the good news: *colleges know there was a worldwide pandemic. Your application will be reviewed within that paradigm.* So, take a breath. I'll address each of the above concerns in the appropriate section of this book, and let you know how you can most effectively pivot to take advantage of those changes.

Now, let's get an overview of what to expect, but remember, I'm outlining a process that usually takes four years to complete, so try not to get overwhelmed. I'll provide specific instructions for each step later in the book. If, as you read through this list, you realize you're behind schedule, don't worry. The process is easy to accelerate. You just have to be disciplined.

A College Planning Timeline: One Year at a Time

Freshman Year

Follow the "Seven Steps to Success" listed above. Two items are worth emphasizing. First, start strong academically. If you're given the opportunity, select a challenging class over an easier one, but make sure you can do well. It's much easier to start and stay strong rather than try to correct a low GPA from a poor freshman year. Also, choose electives that show your interests. Second, plan your summers. Most summer opportunities are publicized in February or March. Think ahead to make the most out of your summer break. If your family takes a summer vacation to an area where several colleges are located, spend a day touring schools. You don't necessarily have to be interested in the institution itself, but visiting a university will open your mind to attributes you may eventually want to consider when looking for a college.

Explore inside and outside the classroom. Let your curiosity guide you into new activities and academics. Sometimes we don't know what we want to do until we experience it.

Start your activities resumé. At this point, it probably won't look like much, but write down (or ask your parents to write down) how you spend your time outside of classes. Everything counts: volunteer work, sports, organizations, competitions, hobbies, employment, etc. Pay particular attention to unique opportunities created by the pandemic. Eventually, when your resumé is put in its final form, you may delete some activities, but for now, include everything. See chapter nine for details about creating a resumé and see this book's appendix for a simple template of a student resumé.

Sophomore Year

Just like freshman year, follow the "Seven Steps to Success" and continue to explore. If you've discovered an area of interest, take your involvement in it to the next level. Use what you've learned to successfully compete, benefit others, or show commitment in that field. Continue building your resumé, but never do something just because it looks good on paper. Explore out of a genuine interest and a desire to learn.

This is the tax year that will determine need-based financial aid eligibility, e.g., if you graduate in May 2024, your 2022 income tax return will determine your student aid index (expected family contribution) and need-based eligibility. Don't worry if you don't know what I'm talking about, but do make sure you and your parents read chapter six to discover how this piece of information can help you pay less for college.

Summer after Sophomore Year

This is the time a student should transition from college awareness to college planning. As I mentioned previously, you may be behind on these assignments, but don't let that scare you. Just move ahead, one step at a time.

Start considering fields of interest as potential majors, but don't be overwhelmed. No one expects a sixteen or seventeen-year-old to know what he wants to do the rest of his life, but hopefully, based on the last two years of exploration, you've noticed a few spheres of interest. Here's the good news: you don't have to know exactly what you want to study, but if you can determine a few target areas, it will be helpful in developing your college criteria (more about that in chapter two).

College is an academic endeavor, but more importantly, it's about transitioning to adulthood and getting the tools you need for your future career. If you already have an area of interest that intrigues you, explore it further. Try to find someone in that field whom you can talk to or shadow. Ask your parents if they know anyone who can help you. Consider what possible majors may prepare you for a career in that field. Read chapter three to find out more about determining your direction.

If you don't have any real areas of interest, try taking some assessments: personality, interest, and aptitude. A lot of research has been done regarding personality types and careers, but additionally, a student should consider his interests and his aptitudes. There are quite a few free assessments online, but you may get additional benefits from some of the reasonably priced, fee-based sites. See my suggestions in chapter three.

If, after you've taken some assessments, you still can't determine areas of interest or potential majors, don't worry. Continue to explore. Most universities allow students to enter as an undeclared major, and many students change their major multiple times during the four years of college. Remember, even when you major in a particular field, you may not work that area for the rest of your life. You will, however, use the transferable tools you gather during your undergraduate years for the rest of your life: tools like critical thinking, communication, and collaboration.

The summer after sophomore year is an ideal time to develop your college criteria. I explain how to do this in chapter two. Determining college criteria is a necessary step in finding a school that will meet your needs. It isn't rocket science, but it does require some introspection. All too often, students are in a hurry and skip this step. Please don't. My primary mantra for college planning is, "It's not about finding a great school. It's about finding a great fit." You won't be able to determine a great fit until you decide what you need. The most common mistake I see in college planning is that people start with the school instead of the student. Take some time to consider what constitutes a good fit for you. Develop your college criteria this summer.

Your college criteria will enable you to create your college list. This can be somewhat time consuming, but if you following the directions in chapter four, you'll be able to develop a list that meets your needs.

Think about your standardized testing schedule. You'll find a lot more information about this topic in chapter seven. Standardized testing causes a huge amount of angst among high school students—as if their entire future depends on their test scores. While that's not entirely true, standardized test scores are important, even with the current increase in test-optional schools. I usually recommend a student take the ACT or SAT and, if the student's score reflects his academic potential, he should submit it. This additional effort shows reflects positively on the student's application. On the other hand, if the student's score is not commensurate with his GPA, he doesn't have to submit a score to a test-optional school. Scheduling your test at the proper time in your academic career can be beneficial. Many students struggle with the math portion of ACT and SAT because, by the time they take the test, they are in calculus or pre-calculus, and they've forgotten some of the concepts covered on the test. Think about where you are in math. Traditionally, a student takes ACT or SAT during spring of his junior year, but if you've completed Geometry, Algebra 1, and Algebra 2, you may find it's easier to take ACT or SAT during fall of your junior year or even the summer before the junior year. Also, consider what else is going on in your life when you schedule your test date. Will you be in a busy athletic season or in the midst of finals? Maybe that's not the best time. Whatever you decide, try to finish your standardized testing prior to your senior year.

Junior Year

Continue to follow the "Seven Steps to Success," bearing in mind this will be the last full academic year that colleges see before you apply. Take everything up a notch. Demonstrate your potential in all areas.

If you haven't already done so, use your college criteria (described in chapter two) to develop an initial college list of between twenty and thirty schools, then research each institution thoroughly. Use third-party sources, student reviews, videos, and the school website itself. Take everything with a grain of salt, and consider the source. Gather information about whatever is important to you, and create questions about things you need to know. Chapter four details the process. Your final list should consist of no more than ten schools with varying degrees of selectivity.

Unless you've already done so, prepare for and take your standardized tests this year (PSAT, ACT and/or SAT, and possibly AP and/or SAT 2).

Get feedback from your guidance counselor on your college list.

Interact with representatives from the schools on your list through phone calls, online visits and admissions sessions, and, once they are allowed again, community visits and college fairs. Ask them questions that will help you further refine your list. Visit as many colleges on your list as you can (assuming universities are able to allow campus visits), ideally when school is in session. Follow the protocol in chapter five to ensure a successful visit.

Find teachers who can give you strong recommendations when you apply to college next fall. Talk to those teachers about your plans and get their feedback on your list of schools.

Summer after Junior Year

Catch up on all aspects of college planning including college visits and last-minute test preparation (if necessary).

Volunteer, work, create, learn, or in some way make the summer productive.

Determine which schools you will apply to and what each school requires to complete its application. Make a list of essay topics, recommendations, and necessary supplemental materials and application deadlines. Investigate scholarships that require additional applications and honors college entrance requirements as needed.

After you know what's necessary, create an application timeline (a schedule) that includes all the tasks you need to complete in order to finish your applications, remembering that many college applications do not open until August 1st. Plan to complete as much as possible before school starts and finish everything by November 1st. Creating and following a realistic timeline is critical to a successful college application process. See my suggestions in chapter nine as well as the required documents sample and application timeline sample in the appendix.

If you will be applying to schools that accept the Common Application (https://commonapp.org), the Coalition Application (https://coalitionforcollegeaccess.org) or the Universal Application (https://www.universalcollegeapp.com/), start the general portion of those applications anytime this summer. These applications generally close for a week in July, but when they come back online August 1st, your information will still be there, and you'll be ahead of the game. Most of the questions are quite basic. You may need to wait until school starts to get some of the school information from your counselor, but do as much as you can this summer. Use the information from your updated resumé to report awards and activities on your applications. Always check the date on individual school applications or supplements so you don't submit last year's application for this year's admission cycle.

Complete your main Common App or Coalition App essay (if applicable). This is an important piece of your application. Chapter nine offers valuable suggestions for this phase.

Senior Year

August 1st is the traditional launch of college application season. I encourage you to hit your applications hard and fast once it opens. It's easy to run out of steam.

Follow the application schedule you previously created and keep track of completed items.

When school starts, do well academically. Avoid senioritis. If a student's grade average falls significantly during the senior year, a university can rescind its offer of admission.

If at all possible, submit all applications and supplements by November 1st. (Many deadlines are later than that, but why drag it out? The sooner you apply, the sooner you can relax.)

A few days after you submit your application to a university, you'll probably receive instructions about how to set up a student account to keep track of that school's application elements. Set up an account at each university so you'll know when your supplemental information is received and your application is complete.

Then, enjoy your senior year!

You should start receiving responses to your applications by mid-December, possibly earlier.

Some families find it useful to make a spreadsheet to compare various aspects of top schools. If your first-choice school is not affordable, you may need to appeal your financial award. I explain this procedure in chapter ten.

Consider your options. During spring break, you may need to visit your top school choices again.

The national deadline for accepting an offer of admission is May 1st, but if you are certain of your decision, you may respond sooner.

Once you make a decision, accept your offer of admission, send in your deposit(s), and sign up for orientation and registration at your future school. Additionally, write a thank-you email to the admissions officer at each school where you've decided not to attend. Thank him for his offer and let him know you've enrolled at another university.

See chapter eleven for tips about transitioning into college.

Chapter 2

You-niversity Utopia Part One

There's no such thing as a perfect school.

I'm sorry if you're disappointed by that piece of information, but it's true. Every institution has pluses and minuses, and ultimately, the student has to decide what aspects are most important to him. Is it cost? Location? The quality of the academics? The athletic program? Student-professor interaction?

Many things go to into choosing the right school for a student, and ultimately, what makes a school right for one student and not right for another are the student's priorities. One of the most effective ways to determine these priorities is through a process called "developing college criteria."

Hundreds of outstanding schools exist in the United States and thousands more worldwide. I have visited many of them, and in every case, I could describe the school as "great." Just because a school is great in general terms, however, doesn't mean the school is great for you. That's why instead of focusing on finding a great school, I encourage students to find a school that's a great fit.

Start with the Student

In order to find a great fit, a student needs to start his college search with some introspection. While that may sound easy, many high schoolers have never taken the time to evaluate their own strengths, weaknesses, aptitudes, passions, and priorities—all of which make the student who he is.

So, where do you begin? How do you determine if a school is a great fit for you?

Start by considering some questions. Before you answer them, you need to know there are no right or wrong answers. You also need to know that you can change your answers at any time. No penalty! But one thing you do need to do is write down your answers. It's interesting to watch your criteria change as you research and visit schools, and it's good to keep track of how your priorities transition.

So, open up a blank document on your computer or get a pad of paper and write the answers to the following questions about Utopia U:

1. How close to home do you want to be? Is it a matter of mileage or ease of transportation? Does it matter?
2. Do you prefer a certain type of weather? Do you like living in a warm climate? Cold? Wet? Four seasons? Does it matter?
3. Do you prefer a particular type of location? Urban? Rural? Large college town? In the United States? International? Does it matter?
4. How important is the environment surrounding your college? Do you enjoy being around mountains? The ocean? Lakes? Forests? Does it matter?
5. What size of class are you most comfortable in? Over 150 students? Fewer than 50? Around 35? Fewer than 20? Why? What size of class do you think would be most conducive to your learning?
6. What is your normal behavior in class? Do you take notes? Listen? Participate in discussion?
7. Do you feel as if you learn best by reading about a topic, discussing a topic, or listening to a lecture on a topic?
8. If you had to do something for a grade, would you prefer to take a test, write a paper, or do a project?
9. On a scale of 1-10, how important is student/professor interaction?

10. On a scale of 1-10, how much academic pressure/competition do you want at the school?
11. What words would you like to describe the students at your college? Studious? Intelligent? Free-spirited? Diverse? Tight-knit? Fun-loving? Balanced? Supportive? Spirited? (Describe the type of culture you'd like to have on your campus.)
12. Do you want a school that is faith-based, and if so, what does that mean to you? Required chapels? Required religion classes? Opportunities to grow spiritually? Bible studies on campus?
13. What are a few things you'd like to do in college, e.g., research with professors, go to football games, study abroad, go on mission trips, belong to a sorority or fraternity, participate in internships, enjoy outdoor activities, perform in theatre, play in a band, be active in intermural sports, etc.?
14. What type of environment do you thrive in? Structured? Independent? Nurturing? Fast-paced? Laid-back?
15. Do you prefer a state school, a private school, or does it matter?
16. How important is the "name" of the school? Is it important that it's prestigious or highly ranked (which usually means it's also more expensive than lesser known but equally excellent schools)?
17. What can your family afford to pay annually? (Ask your parents. Nobody wants to pay for college, but most of us have to.) How much has your family saved for higher education? Are you willing to take out loans? You'll find a lot of information about college costs in chapter six.
18. What is your expected cumulative GPA when you graduate from high school?
19. What is your estimated best test score (ACT/SAT)?
20. Describe your perfect school.
21. Describe your worst school.
22. Do you know what you want to study as a major? Minor? What types of classes would you like offered?

That wasn't so hard, was it?

Now, let's evaluate your answers and what they might mean in terms of criteria.

Questions 1-4: For many students, location is a huge factor. Think about why you answered what you did. If you chose an urban environment because you want to have things to do, remember, most colleges have tons of activities happening on campus, regardless of where the school is located.

If you're thinking you need to be in a large city for internship possibilities or job opportunities, think again. Many times, businesses in a college town consider themselves a part of the campus community and go above and beyond in offering opportunities to students. If you want your campus to have a more traditional feel (lots of greenery and everything within walking distance), you may not find that in a highly urban location. On the other hand, some urban schools do a great job of creating a lush oasis in the middle of a concrete jungle.

If you prefer to stay close to home, remember, college is not thirteenth grade; it's a transition to adulthood. If you want to live at home while attending college, talk to your parents about what this will look like. You and your family may find it easier for you to transition to adulthood if you rent an apartment or a house with friends. If you enroll in a college within an easy driving distance from your home, you may not want to return home every weekend. Certainly, you should occasionally visit your family and friends, but you also need to develop independence.

Questions 5-9: Even if you don't want smaller classes, if you enjoy class discussions, prefer writing papers to taking tests, and look forward to interacting with professors, you may prefer an undergraduate population of under twelve thousand students. A college professor can only stretch himself so far, and in institutions with a population of over twenty thousand students, classes may be so large a professor may not have time to interact as much with each student as he wants. Tests take less time to grade than papers or projects; therefore, large lecture classes tend to rely on tests for grading purposes. Additionally, graduate school applications rely heavily on personal recommendations from professors. If you plan on attending graduate school, you need to remember that relationships with your professors (regardless of the size of your school) are important.

What should you do if you want the spirit and feel of a large school but crave individual attention from professors? One answer is to enroll in the honors college at a large university. Most honors colleges require a student to take a certain number of honors courses while attending the university and complete a capstone project during his senior year. Honors courses usually limit the size of classes to allow for more discussion-based teaching and give students greater access to top teachers who enjoy working with students individually. The classes aren't necessarily harder, but they are more in depth. Honors colleges have separate admission requirements and often require an additional application, essay, or recommendation for admission, but the benefits of early registration, special dorms, and unique opportunities are well worth it. If you don't meet the requirements of an honors college as an incoming freshman, many times, you can apply to the honors college after your first semester or first year on campus (if you have the grades). On the other hand, if you apply to the honors college as an incoming freshman and decide it's not for you, it's usually pretty easy to withdraw from the honors college and continue on the traditional track. If you've been awarded a scholarship specifically for attending the honors college, however, and decide to withdraw, you will forfeit those funds.

Questions 10-14: These questions drill down into the culture and community of the school. This is why it's important that, at some point, you try to visit the schools you're most interested in. (See chapter five.) Researching a school by reading about it and talking about it can only give you so much information. When you visit a school, you get a taste of the culture, the competition, and the community. Know what you want and see if it's demonstrated in the campus culture when you visit.

Questions 15-19: Parents would like to say they can afford every college, but the truth is, many can't. The cost of higher education has risen to extreme levels. While many schools offer valuable institutional scholarships, sometimes the scholarships aren't enough. A family must be wise in determining whether a school is affordable. Cost is an important criterium, and it's addressed in much greater depth in chapter six, but for now, consider these thoughts:

1. A state university will almost always be less expensive than a private institution, even if the public school is not in the student's home state. Many state schools belong to consortiums that offer discounts to residents of neighboring states, so research that as a possibility.
2. Although state schools have a lower price tag, private colleges offer larger scholarships to a higher percentage of students than public universities do. The average merit scholarship for students attending a private university is between twenty-five and forty percent of the tuition. This helps level the playing field between a more expensive private college and a public university. Sometimes families decide the price difference between a large state school and a smaller private institution is so insignificant that it's worth paying more for a better fit.
3. The full cost of college depends on many things, including available scholarships, the four-year graduation rate, accelerated programs, and the treatment of AP and CLEP credits. I'll address more of the differences among schools in chapter six.
4. The more familiar the name of the school is, the more expensive the institution is. It's a basic law of economics: supply and demand. When a school has more applicants than available spots, the school doesn't have to offer as many scholarships because people are willing to pay more to attend a better-known school. Many people mistakenly believe if a school is well-known (usually because of its sports teams), the school itself is better. That's not necessarily true. A strong athletic program doesn't

necessarily mean a strong university. Similarly, some students are overly concerned with rankings. Most of the algorithms that determine school rankings are completely baseless as far as the quality of education. Finally, some students believe that to get a good job or be accepted to graduate school, you have to attend a prestigious school. Most corporations recruit from many schools, not just familiar ones. If you've never heard of a school, it doesn't mean the school is lacking. It simply means you haven't heard of it.

5. You can easily find the average GPA and average test scores for incoming students to a particular institution while researching a school. In order to put yourself at the top of the applicant pool and increase your chances of getting a large scholarship, you should have an above average GPA and test score. A large percentage of students are admitted to their first-choice institutions, however, according to the Higher Education Research Institute,[1] only about a third of students attend their first-choice school, primarily because they don't receive enough scholarship money. In the world of higher education, average is the same distance from good as it is from bad. Be above average.

Questions 20-21: Sometimes a student knows what he doesn't want rather than what he does want. Both are important. As you develop these ideas, think about why certain elements are important to you.

Question 22: Although you don't have to decide on a major before entering college, if you do have several fields that interest you, you can make sure your college offers those choices. Not every school has a college of education, engineering, nursing, or architecture. You can almost always change your major as long as your school offers that choice, and, trust me, it's easier to change your major than change your school.

Your potential college major should play a significant role in your college criteria. In fact, it's so important that the next chapter is all about how to choose your major.

Chapter 3

What Do You Want to Be When You Grow Up?

Choosing a Major Using Assessments

As soon as a child can talk, it's the question he's supposed to know the answer to: What do you want to be when you grow up? With all the concern about his potential profession before a child can even read, is it any wonder students stress over finding the correct answer?

Relax. Most forty-year-olds don't know what they want to be when they grow up, much less a seventeen-year-old. Most of the time, a student doesn't need to know his major when he enters college. Yes, you may be asked that question on a college application, but it's extremely rare that the university will hold you to the answer on your application. In fact, the average student changes his major five times. College is about exploration, and while changing your major isn't necessarily bad, it can cause the student to spend more time in or more money for school. Therefore, in my opinion, a student should start exploring potential career fields (or at least areas of interest) while he is still in high school.

I know it's a big, wide, wonderful world out there, and sometimes students find it scary to limit their choices. Certainly, saying yes to one thing means saying no to another, but the reverse is true as well. You can't do everything, and you weren't meant to either. You have a purpose—a place where your abilities and your desires collide—and that's the sweet spot you're seeking.

High school students should start to explore majors because choosing a field of study (a major) is one of the most important college criteria a student can determine. I'm not saying a student has to know for sure what he wants to study in college, but it is helpful to recognize four or five areas of interest while the student is in high school, and then make sure the colleges on the student's list have several of those majors. As I've mentioned, not every school has a college of education, engineering, or nursing, or a major in anthropology or journalism. If a student does find he's interested in a particular field, he should choose a school that offers that major; otherwise, he's letting the university tell him what he can study rather than determining it himself. A student can only study what the university offers.

Some high school students know exactly what they want to study in college—but those are rare. For the majority, narrowing down interests and determining a major are difficult. Thinking about potential fields requires introspection about aptitudes, talents, prior experiences, and interests. It's easy to become self-absorbed rather than self-aware.

One strategy that's proven highly successful for students to determine areas of interest is taking assessments. I usually recommend a combination of personality, interest, and aptitude assessments.

Personality assessments run the gamut—from the Enneagram to Myers-Briggs to DISC. Many are offered free online or for a small fee. Significant research has been done regarding which personality types are best suited for which jobs.

Even more important than investigating personality, however, is the role aptitudes and interests play in finding a vocation. When it comes to career success, aptitude and interest go hand-in-hand. When someone is interested in something, he works at it, and, therefore, he becomes better at it. When a person becomes better at something, he becomes more interested in it, and the cycle continues. Many aptitude and interest assessments are available online, but my favorite is Youscience (https://www.youscience.com), an online assessment that explores fifteen different aptitudes and six interest areas.

Independent education counselors or school counselors frequently offer assessments as part of their services to students. Generally, after the testing, the counselor explains the results as well as a methodology for continued exploration of the student's areas of interest.

Shadowing

Discovery is a process. Recognizing how your personality, interests, and aptitudes correspond to certain careers is only the first step in discovery. After a student has explored all potential career matches to his personality, interests, and aptitudes, he should choose five to seven areas that sound most interesting, and research which majors might be appropriate for that career.

The next step in determining a potential major/career field is experiential exploration. This involves interviewing or shadowing someone who is working in that career field. Sometimes, a family member knows someone in that job. Other times, the student needs to call an organization that employs people in that vocation. The student should explain why he is calling, and, ideally, set up an appointment with an individual in the career field to find out more about the profession. The student needs to be clear he is only asking for a single appointment. Before the meeting, the student should research the career field and create questions such as: What is a typical day like? What type of skills does a person in this field need to succeed? What type of person would enjoy this job? What is the best thing about this job? What's the worst thing about it? How does a person "climb the ladder" in this career? What do you recommend as a college major in order to be prepared for an entry-level position in this field?

Due to liability concerns and privacy issues, some businesses no longer allow students to shadow on site. If this is the case, invite the individual to coffee and interview the person off site about his career. After the interview, if the student still feels the career field would be interesting, he should explore appropriate majors and determine which ones sound most interesting. The availability of those majors at a student's university then becomes an important part of the student's college criteria.

On the other hand, if, during the interview and shadowing process, a student discovers the job isn't to his liking, he should cross that career off his list and explore other potential areas. While this can seem discouraging, in reality, this is good news. It's better to know now than later.

Time needs to be spent exploring career fields and majors. These are significant pieces of the college criteria puzzle—and they are important to colleges as well.

As I mentioned at the beginning of this chapter, most college applications ask what a student is interested in studying. The most common answer is "unknown" or "undeclared." Will it hurt or help a student's chances of acceptance if he lists a particular major on his application form? That's hard to say. Some schools are looking to increase their population in particular majors, so a student who self-selects that major may have an advantage, but there are no guarantees. On the other hand, some majors may be at capacity at a particular university. In either case, the applicant won't know, so the best advice is to simply be honest. If you have an idea of what you want to study, list it on your application. If you don't know, that's okay.

If you're nervous about making the right decision regarding your major, it helps to think of college as a giant hardware store. You're gathering tools for the job ahead—whatever that may be. It's very rare these days for a person to graduate from college and stay in the same job for the rest of his life. With all the changes in the world, it's pretty certain that at some point, you'll be asked to do something you've never done before. When you receive an opportunity, even if you haven't done it before, if you have a toolbox filled with a skill set that includes critical thinking, analysis, and creativity, you'll be able to do it.

Chapter 4

You-niversity Utopia Part Two

It's All About the Match

You've spent some time thinking about who you are and who you want to be. Now, your goal is to find a school that will facilitate that growth while meeting your academic, social, emotional, and financial needs. If you haven't done so already, take a few minutes to write down your current criteria, and keep them handy as you begin your college search. Notice I said, "current criteria," because those priorities may change during the search process, and if they do, that's okay.

There are thousands of fabulous schools in the world, but it's important to remember you're not just looking for a fabulous school; you're looking for a fabulous fit.

Admissions officers are also looking for fit: students who will succeed at their school. They're looking for diversity within the student body, but they also know the type of student they want. In order for an admissions rep to determine if you're a good fit, he needs to know who you are. That's the job of your college application: to communicate not just your grades and test scores, but who you are and who you want to become.

Sometimes the picture of who you are becomes lost among the facts required for the college application. Therefore, before you go any further, while your self-examination is still fresh on your mind, I want you to write one or two sentences about who you are and who you want to be. For lack of a better term, I'll call it a tag.

The reason I call it a tag is because when an admissions team evaluates a student, the team automatically labels the student with what it sees as the student's primary characteristics, for example: "a kid who has shown a lot of responsibility taking care of his two younger siblings while maintaining a 3.5 average and playing varsity basketball," or "a yearbook editor who also writes articles for her local paper and runs her own business as a website designer," or (not good) "an average student with nothing notable on his resumé."

In order for a student to positively influence the label the admissions team gives him, the student must be intentional in his application. This is where having a tag can help. Students should think of a tag as a thesis statement, a statement that will guide the student's application and helps him communicate who he is to a university.

I know this may sound unimportant, but eventually, this tag will direct every facet of your application. The good news is there's no right or wrong, so have fun with it. It may take a few tries before you find a statement that resonates with you, but in the long run, it will save you time and trouble. Ready?

Start by writing five words that encapsulate who you are, nouns or verbs only. What 'proof' do you have that each of those words describes you, e.g., when have you demonstrated those characteristics? Choose two or three of those words you feel are most representative of you and that you can somehow tie together. Think about if you have a defining personality trait that's important to who you are, e.g., something that plays an important role in who you are such as a particular family situation, background, obstacle, or ability. Tie your descriptive words together with your defining trait to create a sentence that expresses who you are. For example,

I'm proud to be a mathematics nerd and the oldest of five children whose first-generation, immigrant parents taught me the value of never giving up.

I feel the need to be heard, so I enjoy speaking on behalf of those who may not have a voice, whether it's refugees from Central America or a kid who's the victim of cyber-bullying.

As the child of a colonel in the U.S. Air Force, I know how to adapt quickly, obey orders, and cultivate long-distance friendships, the latter of which I do without the use of social media.

This tag doesn't have to be complex; it just has to be you. Ultimately, you'll use this statement to guide you through the application process and help you create a complete, unified portrait of who you are. It may change slightly over time, but ultimately, this sentence is the answer to "who am I?"

After you've completed your tag, you're ready to move on from yourself to your schools.

Developing Your List

Now the search for Utopia U can begin.

There are dozens college search engines on the internet. Some of my favorites include Collegeboard's Big Future (https://collegeboard.org), Collegedata (https://collegedata.com), College Insight (https://college-insight.org), and College Scorecard (https://collegescorecard.ed.gov). Peruse college search engines and find one that appeals to you. Then, begin your search.

1. Look at your college criteria. Choose the two or three that seem most important, for example: location, ACT score, majors.
2. Put those three criteria into the search engine (based on the choices available). Click search. Take note of what schools are selected. These are the ones that meet those criteria.
3. Repeat the process with two or three different criteria. Again, note which schools come up. Some schools may be the same as those that were selected with the first set of criteria, and some may be different. Pay attention to the overlapping schools.

4. Repeat the process until you've put in all your criteria at least one time. Create different combinations with your criteria. The goal is to identify which schools keep being selected based on your choices. Those schools, most likely, will be a good fit for you.

A side note: if your search returns no results, you've probably put in too many criteria. Loosen your parameters. Remember, there is no perfect school; that's why you can't input all your criteria at once. Just choose a few items and see which schools are identified as good matches.

Hopefully, now you see why it's so important to identify your college criteria in the beginning of the college planning process. That's how you determine which schools are on your initial college list. By using criteria, you're able to start your search from the standpoint of the student, not simply schools you've heard of.

Your initial college list should consist of approximately twenty to thirty schools. None of these schools will meet every criterium perfectly, but each school is a potential good fit.

Now, you need to refine your list to ten or fewer schools. Some students wonder why I don't recommend applying to more institutions. Basically, it's because every college application requires time and money, and, ultimately, a student can only attend one university. Therefore, it's beneficial if the student refines his list to ten or fewer schools at this time. Refining your college list begins with researching each school.

A student should research a school for three reasons:
1. To find out information about the school
2. To create questions about the school
3. To determine which schools sound like they are the best fit for you.

As you research each school, write your notes either in an electronic file or a hard file. Many schools are similar to each other, but you're looking for the unique characteristics that make one school a better fit for you than another. It's easy to confuse schools if you don't write the information down. Additionally, if you read valuable information about a school, you can take a picture of it, copy the link, or cut and paste the information into the file. I know it's tedious, but this will help you keep track of the positive and negative aspects of each school, and it's much easier to keep track of it rather than having to go back and search for it again.

Refining Your List

Because school websites are essentially little more than PR from the school, I recommend you start your research from the outside and work inward. In other words, start with third-party research.

1. Go to the library or purchase a copy of *The Fiske Guide*, *Princeton Review's Best Colleges*, or *Colleges That Change Lives* (the latter, if you're looking for a small literal arts college). See if one of those books has a review of the school you are researching. If the school is "less prestigious," it may not be listed in a book. That doesn't mean the school isn't worth researching. On the contrary, it may be a hidden gem of a school. Instead google "review of (name of school)." Many websites post college reviews. Bear in mind that some websites are written by current and former students, so the reviews may not be entirely objective. Read what is written about the school and note anything that seems interesting (positive or negative) about the school.
2. Go to collegedata.com (https://collegedata.com)and look at the statistics on the school: cost, size, graduation rate, etc. Is the school still a good possibility according to your criteria?
3. See if you can find a video of the university you are researching on youniversitytv.com (https://youniversitytv.com). Warning: these videos are marketing videos, and you may find the style a little over-the-top. If you can't find a video on youniversitytv, google "virtual tour (name of school)" or look for pictures of the campus on google images (https://images.google.com).

4. If the school still looks intriguing, check out the school's website. Peruse the school's website for whatever you're interested in. Most students are curious about the opportunities available in their potential majors. Some want to check out information about Greek life. Others check out the athletics. Again, as you explore each school, continue to take notes.
5. After you've researched three or four schools, you'll start to get an idea of which schools appeal to you. Start refining your college list by eliminating schools that don't seem as interesting as others. Continue to research all the schools on your initial list, keeping the ones you think are the better fits and removing the others. Your goal is to create a list of ten or fewer schools that seem to fit your criteria best. It's important that your list of schools includes a range of selectivity. Ideally, you want two or three "foundation" schools (sometimes called a "safety" school): schools where you know you'll get accepted and you know you can afford. You also want several target schools: schools that offer a few more opportunities and are closer to your ideal. Check your eligibility for scholarships at these schools because these schools are probably a little more expensive. Finally, you should have a couple of reach schools on your list: the drool schools—the schools where you'd love to go if you could get in and if you could afford them. Sometimes families believe a student shouldn't apply to reach schools because they're so expensive. Yes, these schools are costly, but occasionally, these well-known, well-endowed universities are able to offer students such large scholarships that the actual out-of-pocket cost is fairly reasonable. The trick, however, is being a strong enough applicant to get admitted to these schools.

This is a long, tedious process, but it's important. If your time is limited, consider using an independent education counselor to assist you. An independent counselor can save you a lot of time, especially in the college search process. Do, however, make sure the counselor is a member of at least one professional organization; Higher Education Consultants Association (https://hecaonline.org) or Independent Education Consultants Association (https://iecaonline.org).

Creating Questions

After you've researched your schools and refined your list, it's time to create a set of about ten questions you can ask each school representative. A school representative, a.k.a. admissions counselor, AC, college rep, or admissions rep, is a person whose job is to get to know a certain pool of applicants in order to determine if a student is a good fit for a school. (Just like students search for colleges that are a good fit, college admissions counselors look for students who are a good fit because those are the students who have a higher chance of success at that school.) Usually, students are assigned to a particular admissions counselor based on the physical location of the student's high school.

How do colleges decide if you're a good fit, and what do the ten questions have to do with that? When you submit your application, a college admissions team will assess you, just like you've assessed their university. As you know, however, there's much more to you than your GPA, test scores, essay, and application. In the same way, there's more to a university than what's written on its website. The ten questions are a tool to help you discover additional information about each school, determine differences between the schools on your list, and allow each admissions representative to know more about you.

What types of questions should you ask? That depends on what you're interested in. Remember, however, the types of questions you ask will say a lot about who you are. Go back to the tag you created at the beginning of this chapter and make sure some of your questions address the needs inherent in that statement.

Many students ask about hands-on opportunities in their potential majors or what minors might complement a particular field of study. Others inquire about the requirements and benefits of an honors program. Some want to know about research opportunities or the level of interaction between professors and students. If a student is undeclared, he may ask about advising resources. If he's homeschooled, he should ask about additional admission requirements for homeschoolers. Other students want to know about athletic recruiting, extracurricular activities, or Greek life. The list is as varied as a student's interests.

Craft your questions in the form of conversation starters between you and each admissions representative. Instead of asking questions that have a yes or no answer or are easily answerable on the college website, ask questions that require a narrative as an answer. For example, instead of asking, "Do you have internships?" say, "Can you tell me a little about your hands-on learning opportunities like internships?" Instead of saying, "Do you have an honors program?" say, "Can you tell me about the benefits and requirements of your honors program?" Instead of asking, "Do you have a study abroad program?" ask, "How is study abroad incorporated into the xxx major?"

Think about what's important to you. You may already have an idea of the answer because, after all, you've done the research. Asking a specific question, however, allows you to go deeper and serves as a way for the admissions rep to get to know you and what you care about.

Type up the ten questions you'll ask your admissions counselor at each school. If you haven't done so already, create an electronic or a hard copy file for each school on your list (suggested earlier in this chapter), and put one list of questions in each file. If you have specific questions about a school (usually regarding a particular opportunity or a unique program), include those questions on your list for that school.

You can also create a list of questions to ask your student tour guide at each school, such as: Have you ever had a problem getting classes? What's the campus like on the weekends? How does a student get involved? How has this school changed you? What part does (Greek life/sports/religion) play in the campus culture?

What are three words you'd use to describe this school? Again, ask about whatever matters to you.

Now that you're armed with your research and your questions, you're ready for the next step: forming a relationship with each university on your list.

Chapter 5

Getting to Know You

Although it's actually quite simple, this next step in college planning often proves exceptionally difficult for today's high school students: talking to admissions counselors. This often-overlooked action can be the difference between acceptance and denial at a university or no money and enough money to make a private college affordable.

Based on your research, you now know what schools are a good fit for you. The admissions counselors at those institutions, however, don't know that you're a great fit for them. That's why you have to form a relationship with each of your schools' admissions counselors: to give them a chance to get to know you.

Although speaking to an admissions counselor is probably out of your comfort zone, if you have questions (like the list I suggested you create in the last chapter), the conversation is significantly less stressful. When you ask an admissions representative to talk about his school, you'll gain insight into the institution, but you'll also display traits that most admissions counselors are looking for in potential students:

- you've done your research.
- you're interested in the school.
- you're a student who takes initiative.
- you know hard work has a reward.

Those are the characteristics that, to an admissions representative, spell success.

A word on timing: A one-on-one conversation with an admissions representative, whether it's via phone or in person, is always more beneficial for the student if it occurs before a student submits his application. That way, the admissions representative has personal knowledge of you before he considers your application. That's usually a big plus.

Prospective Student Experiences

In the pre-pandemic days, forming a relationship with an admissions rep was fairly straightforward: create questions, make a phone call, attend the admissions rep's presentation when he visits your high school, and ultimately, visit campus. During the pandemic, however, many campuses closed to visitors, so the game changed.

This was not necessarily a bad thing. In fact, many universities significantly improved their online opportunities for prospective students. Even after campuses re-open, students should continue to take advantage of these enhanced online visits in addition to the in-person visits.

Opportunities for prospective students vary from school to school. In order to find out what online tools are available to you, google the name of a particular school followed by the words "virtual visit." It may take a little detective work, but eventually you'll discover what's available. Some schools offer only pre-recorded tours and information sessions; others provide live tours, interviews, and sessions with professors. Take advantage of every opportunity.

Virtual Visits

Some students prefer doing virtual visits prior to contacting their admissions reps; others do it afterwards. If possible, I recommend participating in a virtual visit prior to speaking to your admissions rep one-on-one. If you participate in virtual experiences (information sessions, tours, departmental presentations) before you speak to your admissions rep, you have more information about the school which could lead to a more robust conversation and more specific questions. Plus, you'll appear more interested than the average student because when the admissions rep asks if you've done a virtual visit (which he's sure to ask), you'll be able to say you have.

Realistically speaking, however, some students are so busy they delay the virtual visits which also postpones the individual phone call. Don't do that. If time is tight, opt for the one-on-one phone call in the spring of your junior year rather than waiting until you've completed your virtual experiences and perhaps not contacting your admissions representative until late summer or early fall. You can always participate in virtual experiences after you've spoken to your admissions representative.

The Phone Call

1. Go online to each school's website and locate the phone number of the admissions office. With your list of ten questions in front of you (and a pencil to take notes), call the phone number of an admissions office and say, "Hi. My name is xxxx. I am a senior (or junior) attending xxxx high school in (city, state). I am researching xxxx (name of college) online and have a few questions. Is there an admission representative available who could answer a few questions for me?" Usually, there will be (although occasionally, the representative will have to call you back). When you are connected with the admissions representative, write down that person's name and introduce yourself again: "Hi. My name is xxxx. I am a rising senior (or junior) attending xxxx high school in (city, state). I am researching xxxx (name of college) online and have a few questions. Can you help me?"
2. The phone call should take a natural progression after that. Ask four or five of your open-ended questions that you consider important. Take notes on your sheet of paper with the questions.

3. If you're planning on visiting the school (I'll explain how to do that later in this chapter) and have already booked that visit online but were unable to schedule a meeting with an admissions counselor, after you've asked several questions, say: "I'm planning on visiting xxx on (date). Would it be possible, while I'm on campus, to have a face-to-face interview with you or another admissions representative to discuss additional questions?" (You may also want to ask about taking a departmental tour, sitting in on a class, meeting with a coach, etc.—anything you weren't able to schedule online.)
4. If you cannot visit the school before you submit your application, you should ask, "Will a representative from (name of school) be in (name of your town) this fall for the college fair or perhaps later this spring? If so, will you be having a presentation I can attend or could I set up a personal interview to get other questions answered?" (During the pandemic, these opportunities ceased, but as the world re-opens, representatives should start visiting again.)
5. When you are finished asking four or five questions, say something like, "Thank you for answering my questions. At this point, that's all I have, but I'm sure I'll come up with more questions over time (which is true because you actually already have those questions prepared. Remember, you only asked half of the questions you have during this phone call.).
6. Close the conversation by saying, "May I get your email address so I can contact you again if I need to?" (Get the email address.) "Thank you so much. I look forward to meeting you/speaking with you again soon."
7. After you hang up, send a brief email to the admissions counselor thanking him for taking the time to answer your questions.
8. Some admissions representatives prefer scheduling and utilizing Skype, Zoom, or Facetime instead of having a good, old-fashioned phone call. If that's the case, that's fine. Just make sure the computer or phone is positioned well (no nostril shots) and you're dressed appropriately for the call.

That wasn't so hard, was it? A phone call can really give your application a boost. Of course, there are no guarantees, but taking the time to let the admissions counselor speak to you, even if it's just over the phone, speaks volumes about the type of person you are.

Fortunately, phone calls are fairly easy to do. They usually take no more than ten minutes, so it's a small investment for a potentially large payback.

If you liked what you heard on the phone, the next step is to further explore the school. First, make sure you've taken advantage of all online opportunities for prospective students. (See the section "Virtual Visits" earlier in this chapter.) Then, schedule an in-person visit to campus. Yes, visiting a school does require time and money, but it is well worth the investment.

Do you have to visit each school on your list? No. However, the chances of your attending a school you don't actually visit are very slim. How do you know if a school is a good fit if you never "try it on?" Visiting a school is your opportunity to get an accurate idea of how well you fit at a particular college or university. It's also important because, when you visit, you may see that you're wrong about a certain piece of criteria. Maybe you decide you don't like big schools or urban settings, but you thought you did. If you visit a college and realize your criteria is wrong, you can stop and take a step backwards (change your preferences and perhaps adjust your list) before you move forward, possibly in the wrong direction. That's right. Switch it up. Adjust your criteria and your school list accordingly. I know it's a lot of trouble, but it's better to do it now and make sure you get a good result rather than doing it later after you realize none of your schools is a good fit.

Even if your actual criteria don't change, your priorities may shift. You may decide that distance from home is more important than the size of your classes or dorm configurations are more important than meal plans. Remember, this is your opportunity to discover what you need—and it's your school. You don't have to fit into anyone else's mold. A good fit for you won't look the same as a good fit for anyone else—not even your parents. With that in mind, let's move on to college visits—the best way to find your fit.

Planning the Visit

Visiting colleges is an important part of the college planning process. If possible, visit a school while it is in session (not during break). I realize this may be impossible, and if that's the case, a visit during a school break is better than no visit at all. I also recommend visiting more than one school in a trip because, although your schools may all be good fits, as you compare one school to another, you'll begin to rank your schools in your head—and that's a vital piece of the final decision (plus it's less expensive to visit multiple schools in one trip).

Most aspects of college planning need to be performed by the student, however, because college visits involve financial and logistical preparation, the parent needs to be involved in scheduling visits. The parent can book visits online, but during the actual visit (or if the planning process requires any phone calls to the admissions office), the student should take the lead.

1. A month or two before you plan on visiting, google "visit (name of school)." (School visits can get filled, so I don't advise waiting until the last moment to reserve a tour, plus if you have to fly, ticket prices and car rental prices are usually more reasonable if you book them farther in advance.) A webpage should pop up that describes the type of visits the college offers (virtual, in-person, group, daily). I almost always recommend booking an individual day visit (tour and information session) because students don't really get noticed on crowded preview days (although if, because of scheduling, you can only do a group visit, you certainly may). Check the days and times individual visits are available for each school. Before you (the parent) book anything, check the visit times for all your schools as well as the drive time between the schools. Determine the most efficient use of your time, but remember, you may need to add some time outside the visit window for a student's interview.

2. After you have a plan (and this may include checking flight times), reserve your visits. I recommend signing up for a tour, information session (sometimes combined), and counselor interview. Sometimes, other opportunities are available such as meeting with someone from the honors college, sitting in on a class, touring a specific department, having lunch on campus, or staying overnight. If you can't sign up online for a counselor interview (or something else you really want to do), the student should call the admissions office after the tour is booked and ask if he can do what he wants to in order to research the school. Highly selective schools may not allow admissions counselor interviews, but sometimes, the school will provide the opportunity for an alumnus to interview the student at a later time. Every school has its own protocol, so ask.
3. Usually, the school will send a confirmation email. Read it when you get it, and make sure you understand where and when you are to meet, where you can park, and whether you need a parking pass. Sometimes the confirmation email includes links to dining coupons or discounts for nearby hotels.
4. Take a few days to finish planning. It is possible to visit two schools in one day if the schools are fairly close together, but it is exhausting. Make sure your family has time to enjoy the evenings so you can look at each school with anticipation rather than exhaustion. If time allows, plan some down time every two or three days during your college visit trip.
5. Shortly before the school visit, the student should review the university's website, his notes about the school, and the questions he wants to ask the admissions counselor (as well as possibly questions for the tour guide—for a student's view of the school). Additionally, the student should determine how he would answer questions he might be asked. Such questions include: Why are you interested in this school? What do you want to study here and why? And the most dreaded "non-question" of all: Tell

me a little about yourself. (Create a one-minute or less "elevator speech" that addresses your interests and goals as they pertain to college.)
6. Some students create a list to remind them of things they want to investigate during their campus visits: dorm options, food, local activities, social life, transportation, etc. I recommend writing all those things down and keeping them with you as you tour campus. Alternatively, you can use the Campus Chronicle form that's included in the appendix of this book.

On Campus

Arrive early for your campus visit. You'll probably be stressed anyway, and the last thing you need is additional worry about finding a parking place or how to find the visitor's center.

While on campus, the student should take the lead. Certainly, parents can ask questions during the tour or information session, but it's best if the student asks most of them. (Parents and students may want to discuss questions beforehand.) Parents and students should both take notes while on campus because it's very easy to confuse schools. Use a journal, notecards, or the Campus Chronicle form in the appendix.

Important: Both the student and the parents (and siblings) should hold opinions (both good and bad) to themselves while on campus and should not elbow each other or comment how something is better or worse than it is at another school. Allow the student to make his own determination about the school. After all, he's the one who will be attending. Parents will eventually have the opportunity to contribute ideas after the student has a chance to process the visit.

The admission interview generally involves the student only. The student can use his notes to remind himself of the questions he wants to ask, and he should write down the admission counselor's answers. While the student is in his admissions interview, parents may want to visit the financial aid office to get an "early read" on possible aid. (Have your student's GPA, test scores, and your EFC available. See chapter six for information on the EFC.) Alternatively, parents can wait at the bookstore or student union, and the family can reconnect after the student completes his interview. Give the student the opportunity to evaluate the school without the pressure of parents asking, "What did you think?"

Don't discuss the school at all until the student takes some time to process the visit.

After the family has left campus and the student has looked at his notes and summarized his thoughts, the student should share his thoughts about the school with his parents (without interruption). After the student finishes talking, the parents should offer feedback and discuss pros and cons. Ultimately, the family should come to a general consensus about whether the school will stay on the list.

What If I Can't Visit?

Ideally, forming a relationship with a school should be a combination of phone calls, virtual visits, and in-person visits, but sometimes the reality is much more challenging. After all, visiting colleges is expensive, and sometimes families can't afford to visit every school. What should happen then?

If possible, try to visit your top three schools. Combine a college visit with a parent's business trip or a vacation.

If you can't visit, double down on the phone calls. I don't want you to harass anyone, but you really do need to have a good feel for the school in order to seriously consider attending it. Make sure you've reached out to your admissions counselor at each university at least twice (plus you should write thank you emails or notes after each contact).

During your first phone call, ask if an admissions counselor will be in your area during the year. If an admissions counselor will be in your area, try to set up a one-on-one interview with the counselor to ask some of the questions you created.

Remember, the purpose of forming a relationship with each admissions representative isn't just for you to learn about the school; it's also for the school representative to get to know you.

That being said, let's remember one important thing about higher education: it's a business. The ultimate job of an admissions counselor is to find students who are a good fit for the school and encourage them to enroll. That's why, when you're talking to an admissions representative, you might get the idea that the school is perfect. It's not. Every university I've visited in the last decade (and there are hundreds) is a great school—for certain students. Hence my mantra: "It's not about finding a great school; it's about finding a great fit."

What does that have to do with visiting a university? Well, sometimes, you get the sense that the admissions counselor is trying a little too hard to sell his school. If that's the case, you might want to ask if you can speak to a student who is currently studying what you're thinking about studying. Certainly, the student will be handpicked—someone who's quite happy and very successful—but most students remember the challenge of trying to discover the truth about a school, so they'll be a little more objective.

In other words, if you can't visit a school before you apply, do everything in your power to get to know it from a distance.

Some families who are on a tight budget intentionally wait to visit the school until after the student has been accepted. Their finances are so lean, they don't want to "waste" a visit to a school where the student isn't accepted. While I do understand this philosophy, it's a bit of a Catch-22.

If a college is semi-selective (it admits fewer than 50% of its applicants), the chance of a student who has visited being admitted is much higher than the chance of a student who has not visited—particularly if the student took the time to speak with an admissions representative while he was on campus.

Colleges have limited places and a limited pocketbook. Colleges tend to admit and financially reward students who have shown interest in them. After all, if a student isn't interested enough in a school to drive eight hours or spend several hundred dollars on an airline ticket, what are the chances of that student actually attending that school? Not very high. Schools want to admit and offer money to students most likely to accept their offer. If a student makes the effort to visit a school and speak to an admissions counselor, it speaks very highly of the student's desire to attend that school. When it's time for the admissions committee to make its decisions, the student's admissions counselor will be able to advocate for the student whom he has met.

Occasionally, if a student speaks honestly to his admissions counselor and expresses the desire to visit, but admits he doesn't have the funds, the admissions counselor can arrange to reimburse the student for a portion of his travel expenses. This is fairly unusual, however, and only happens in extreme circumstances.

Yes, it makes sense financially to wait to visit a school until the student is accepted, but the student may not get accepted if he doesn't visit the school. Sadly, there are no guarantees either way.

Visiting college campuses can be costly and challenging, but the difficulty goes to a whole new level if the student is required to have an interview on campus for a particular scholarship or to audition for a music or theatre program. A family can avoid this problem by planning ahead. If the student wants to enroll in a program that requires an on-campus audition, the student should try to combine his school visit with his audition. Likewise, if a student is required to visit campus for an honors competition or scholarship interview, he should come a day early to do a standard campus visit as well.

Forming a relationship with your college admissions counselor is a critical piece of the college planning process. It requires planning, organizing, money, time, and often, anxiety. Phone calls and interviews with strangers are way out of most students' comfort zones, but it's worth it. Make the effort to get to know everything you can about a university where you might spend the next four years—and let the admissions counselors get to know you.

Chapter 6

Show Me the Money

If you think visiting a university is expensive, try paying for tuition, room, board, books, and fees. Other than purchasing a house, the biggest investment a person will most likely ever make is purchasing a higher education (his or his children's). And that's the right way to look at it. College is an investment—in time, money, and resources. The return can be exponential if a student takes advantages of the opportunities presented to him at college, but the upfront cost is significant.

Regarding college costs, first, let's hear the bad news. In 2018, Forbes Magazine reported that over the last seven years, tuition rose eight times faster than wages did. [2]According to the College Board, in that same year, the average full cost of annual attendance at a public, in-state university was $21,370; the price of a public, out-of-state school was $37,430; and the average full cost of attendance at a private college was $48,510. Those prices include average tuition of $10,230, $26,230, and $35,830 respectively, as well as room, board, books, fees, transportation, and miscellaneous costs. And those numbers are average.[3] Sadly, while seventy-seven percent of students get accepted to their first-choice institution, far fewer actually enroll because of cost.[4]

But now, the good news: Only twelve percent of students pay the full cost of attendance, and most of those are international students.[5] The average tuition discount, i.e., automatic renewable four-year merit scholarship based purely on grades and test scores, at private institutions is fifty-six percent, and the average tuition discount at public schools is approximately $6,500.

Why do private colleges offer so much more money? They know their prices are ridiculous, and they're trying to level the playing field. Few families are willing to pay twenty to thirty thousand dollars more per year for a private rather than public college education, but many will pay five to ten thousand dollars more.

So, how much should you plan on paying for college? That depends. In 2016, most of my clients paid less than twenty thousand dollars per year for an undergraduate education. In 2020, most will pay between twenty-five and thirty thousand dollars per year (and those students have scholarships). Granted, the price tags of these schools are closer to sixty thousand dollars per year, but my point is the price of higher education has gone through the roof. Yes, you can still find strong educational choices for under twenty thousand dollars annually, but every year, the availability decreases.

As a society, we've helped perpetuate the myth that the more expensive the school, the better, and that's not necessarily true. Nevertheless, many colleges raise tuition annually to maintain with their reputation as a good school. One mistake many students make in finding an affordable school is looking for colleges with "names." There are thousands of four-year institutions in the United States (many you've never heard of) that have outstanding programs. Attending a school that is still "under the radar" but has excellent educational opportunities can mean big savings for families.

If a student is fortunate enough to have access to over a hundred thousand dollars for his college education (and is willing to spend it), it doesn't necessarily mean that student will get a better education than the student who doesn't have as much money. It just means the former has more options.

In a nutshell, in-state, public institutions are usually the least expensive option for a student and, generally speaking, easiest to get into—especially those non-flagship institutions. Public, out-of-state schools are slightly more competitive and costly. The most expensive option, at least as far as the price tag is concerned, is always a private institution. Some private colleges, however, offer such good scholarships, their out-of-pocket cost may actually end up being less than an out-of-state, public school and occasionally even the in-state, public school.

So, what's a student to do? Regardless of the price tag of the school or how much the student pays, college must be affordable. What's affordable? Every person's answer is different, and how to pay for college is an issue that must be discussed within a family. It should not include dipping into the parents' retirement savings, but more than likely will entail using money that's been saved specifically for higher education. (See more about this topic under "Other Financial Considerations" below.) I don't pretend to have the answer, but hopefully the information below will help you make the right decision. Please note: rules regarding financial aid and scholarships change frequently. The information below should be verified by the user. I am not a financial advisor, nor do I claim to be. Such professionals exist, but families should make sure the advisor has a specialty in college financial planning. The average financial planner or accountant may not be aware of all the regulations, some of which are extremely complicated. Some college financial planners are excellent and well worth their fees; others are not.

With all this in mind, how can families afford the rising cost of college? One answer is OPM: other people's money, better known as scholarships.

Scholarships and Financial Aid

The topic of college affordability tends to be very confusing. In this book, I will address affordability primarily in terms of financial aid and scholarships.

There are two general categories of financial aid and scholarships: merit-based and need-based. The term financial aid usually denotes loans and work study, money that is either borrowed or earned. The term scholarship (or grant) refers to money that does not have to be repaid. Some universities offer more need-based money; others offer more merit-based money: it depends on the school's policies and goals.

Need-Based Money: FAFSA and the EFC

A student's eligibility for need-based money, either in terms of financial aid or grants and scholarships, is determined by the family's financial situation. A significant amount of need-based aid comes from federal and state governments, but institutions provide need-based money as well.

To obtain need-based money, the parent of a student and the student himself must apply for federal student aid ID numbers (https://studentaid.ed.gov/sa/fafsa/filling-out/fsaid). Then, the parent (or the student) completes an online form called FAFSA, the Free Application for Federal Student Aid (https://studentaid.gov/h/apply-for-aid/fafsa).

This form, which opens on October 1st every year, gathers information about a family's income and assets.

A family should complete a FAFSA during the fall of the student's senior year. Many schools require FAFSA to be submitted before making its admissions decision; therefore, a student should be aware that different schools have different deadlines for FAFSA. Because so much need-based money is tied to federal or state governments, FAFSA is linked to a Data Retrieval System through the Internal Revenue Service. This means once a parent inputs his social security number, part of his financial information is automatically populated based on two years' prior taxes. In other words, if a student is applying for a college term that begins in August of 2023, the financial information for the FAFSA is based the parents' 2021 tax year (and the student's if the student filed taxes).

Other information such as the current balance of a checking account or the value of a family's investments should be based on the day the form is submitted. Since having less money in the bank or in investments makes a student more eligible for need-based aid, some parents submit the FAFSA on a day the stock market drops or immediately after a large bill has been paid (e.g., does the student need a new computer as an early graduation gift?).

If a family's financial situation changed significantly in the last two years (which certainly happened during the pandemic), and the information on the two years' prior tax return is no longer relevant, parents can contact each school and, once evidence is provided, the school will update the financial information.

The algorithm used to calculate financial aid through FAFSA is extremely complicated. Basically, the government has determined, based on a family's income, assets, size, age of older parent, location, and a multitude of other factors, how much a family should pay for higher education. This amount is called the EFC, an abbreviation for Expected Family Contribution. (Note: This term is set to change to SAI/Student Aid Index sometime in 2022 for applications for the 2023-2024 academic school year when FAFSA goes through a "simplification process.") A few key aspects of the calculation of the EFC are:

1. The government allows a financial exemption for each family based on several factors. The exempted funds are not included in the calculation of a family's EFC, but all other income and assets are included in the determination of the EFC. The exemption is usually quite small—usually, just enough for the family to afford essentials.
2. Generally speaking, parents are expected to pay somewhere between five and six percent of their combined income and assets for every year of college.
3. Students are expected to pay approximately twenty percent of their income and assets for every year of college.
4. In light of the rules regarding eligibility for need-based aid, it's always wiser for parents to save under their name rather than the student's.
5. Parents can estimate their expected family contribution at fafsa4caster.com. (https://fafsa.ed.gov/spa/fafsa4c/?locale=en_US&_ga=2.234618012.387921916.1570364456-1511083644.1570364456 - /landing) A family should do this well before the student applies to college to predict the possibility of need-based aid.

Once a family knows its Expected Family Contribution (a.k.a. Student Aid Index) (which is always higher than parents hope it will be), eligibility for need-based scholarships and financial aid can be estimated for each school. Eligibility for need-based aid is determined by subtracting a family's EFC/SAI from a school's total cost of attendance (usually listed on the school's website). Therefore, the more expensive the school, the higher the likelihood of the student's eligibility for need-based aid.

The report that is generated to determine the EFC is called the SAR (Student Aid Report). Once a family inputs its information, the SAR is generated and is sent for free (hence, the name, Free Application for Federal Student Aid) to ten schools on the student's list. If a student applies to more than ten schools, after the initial report is generated, a parent can delete some of the schools on the FAFSA and replace them with names of other institutions.

Currently, if a family has more than one student attending college simultaneously, the EFC is distributed among the students on each student's Student Aid Report. For example, if a family's EFC is $30,000 per year and the family has two students in college, each student's EFC is $15,000. Because each student's individual EFC is lower, each student should be more eligible for need-based aid. This will no longer be true after the FAFSA is simplified when the full SAI (EFC) will be applied to each student.

After FAFSA is submitted and the Student Aid Report generated, each school on the student's college list has access to the family's financial information and will determine the possibility of federal need-based aid as well as institutional or state need-based aid. Note: A school is not obligated to meet a student's total need. In fact, different schools meet different percentages of a student's need, ranging from thirty to one hundred percent. Both the amount and the way in which a school chooses to meet the financial need of its students are entirely up to the school. The university may offer need-based aid in terms of government funds, institutional funds, or a combination of both.

Loans

One of the most common ways students receive need-based aid is through the Federal Direct Loan Program. Operated by the U.S. Department of Education, this program offers loans to students while they are in college. In order to help students not become over extended, the program limits its loan amounts. At the time of publication, those limits are $5500 per year for freshmen, $6500 per year for sophomores and juniors, and $7500 per year for seniors. A federal loan may be subsidized (no interest accrues until the student graduates) or unsubsidized (interest accrues as soon as the money is disbursed). The loan is taken out under the student's name at a very reasonable interest rate (usually between four and six percent). Several repayment options are available and should be researched by the family. Additionally, loan forgiveness programs are possible for students entering fields such as education, medicine, and public service (https://studentaid.gov/manage-loans/forgiveness-cancellation).

Whether a student takes out an educational loan is the decision of the student and his family. Some families try to avoid all debt; others find it necessary to borrow money to afford higher education. Like all lenders, the federal government expects these loans to be fully repaid—except in extremely rare circumstances. A general rule of thumb is that, if a student chooses to take out a loan, he should borrow no more than what he estimates his income will be during his first year of full-time employment.

One way some families use student loans is that, if the student maintains good grades, the family repays the loan. If the student does not live up to his academic potential, the student repays the loan. Many families find money is a strong motivation for academic excellence.

Other Forms of Need-Based Aid

Another way students receive need-based aid is through the Federal Work Study Program. Students apply for and work various jobs on campus and get paid an hourly wage. One thing to note about the Work Study Program is that the funds the students receive are usually not applied to the actual cost of college; rather, they are used for pocket money.

Students can also receive need-based aid through institutional grants or the Federal Pell Grant. These grants are usually given to the most needy students, and do not have to be repaid (https://studentaid.gov/understand-aid/types/grants/pell).

Universities usually offer a combination of loans, grants, and work study funds to provide need-based aid. A few of the most selective schools cap or no longer include loans as part of the financial aid package if a family's income is under a certain amount. These schools are usually considered need-blind institutions. As long as the student is admitted, the school will meet one hundred percent of the financial need. The challenge in this situation is actually being admitted.

Additional Issues in Need-Based Aid

In addition to FAFSA, a few hundred highly selective schools require the CSS Profile. This is a form produced by the College Board that explores a family's finances more thoroughly, and it does cost to file. Some schools use the CSS Profile not only to determine need-based aid but merit-based aid as well. If a student's parents are divorced, some CSS Profile institutions require both parents (custodial and non-custodial) complete a portion of the form. Conversely, FAFSA-only schools never consider the non-custodial parent's finances. A student should check the requirements of each school. (Note: When it updates in 2022, FAFSA will require the parent who provides the most financial support to complete the FAFSA, regardless of which parent the student lives with or who claims the student on taxes.)

Many parents dread completing FAFSA and the CSS profile, but as I tell my students when they are studying for standardized tests, "calculate the potential hourly wage." For many families, the one to four hours spent completing these forms result in tens of thousands of dollars.

It is true some families will not qualify for need-based aid, and the time spent won't reap financial benefits. Still, I almost always recommend a family spend a couple of hours completing the necessary forms (FAFSA and/or CSS Profile) in case the student is eligible. Like so many things, you don't know until you try.

To summarize about need-based aid and the FAFSA:

1. Whether you qualify for need-based aid depends on the price of the school. The more expensive the school, the more likely the student will qualify for aid.
2. Different schools meet different percentages of need. Some schools meet one hundred percent of need. Other schools meet considerably less need, with an average range of forty to sixty percent. A university is not required to meet any particular degree of need.
3. Some schools require a student's FAFSA be submitted before the student is eligible for any scholarships or financial aid: merit-based or need-based. Most colleges require a FAFSA before considering the student for need-based assistance.
4. If a family is considering not completing the FAFSA, verify that the institution will consider a student's application complete without it.
5. A student's degree of eligibility for need-based aid can change from year to year depending on a family's financial situation. Therefore, if a student receives any federal aid as a freshman, the family needs to update the FAFSA annually. It is possible that if a student isn't eligible for need-based aid one year, he may be eligible another year due to a change in circumstances.

Merit-Based Money

Merit-based money operates differently from need-based aid and is used primarily by universities in four ways:

1. Provides a tuition discount so the university is more affordable and, thus, more attractive for students who might otherwise prefer schools with a lower price tag. In other words, it helps level the playing field regarding cost among institutions.
2. Offers money to students with particular characteristics (e.g., geographic origin, specific talents, grade point/test scores) to attract the type of student the school desires. (This is called enrollment management. You can read more about this practice below.)
3. Gives a student "bragging rights" that he was offered a certain amount of money because the university found him a desirable candidate, thus, in the student's mind, creating a more positive view of the school. (While this may indeed be true, many times, a merit scholarship is simply a standard tuition discount—offered to over ninety-five percent of applicants.)
4. Helps fill beds. Let's face it: cost of attendance is a major consideration for many families. The more affordable a school is, the more likely a student is to matriculate.

Every school has different standards for providing merit-based money. Some schools require a specific GPA, test score, or, in the case of many large schools who try to be straight forward in their financial offers, a combination of both. (I call it chart-based money.) In other words, "x" GPA plus "y" test score equals "z" money (although during the pandemic, many schools dropped the test score requirement). Other schools utilize a strategy called "enrollment management," a policy in which an institution offers additional funds (usually scholarships or grants) to students who possess certain characteristics. For example, some universities offer National Merit Finalists full tuition scholarships; other colleges give significant amounts of money to athletes or musicians, and others may provide substantial grants to particular minority groups. Some institutions award money simply as a response to a student submitting his application, when, in reality, this has nothing to do with merit and everything to do the school using a tuition discount to gain favor in an applicant's mind.

Most universities don't require an additional application for merit-based scholarships. They consider a student's application for admission as the scholarship application. A few schools, however, require students to enter information into a school-based scholarship database in order to apply for endowed scholarships for which they are eligible. Some universities offer large, highly competitive scholarships to its top applicants. Many times, these scholarships require additional applications, essays, recommendations, and/or on-campus interviews. While these competitive scholarships do require extra effort, the payoff is often a four-year, full-tuition scholarship or sometimes even more. These additional scholarships may or may not be dependent on admission to the university's honors program or honors college. If a student is thinks he may be eligible for top scholarships at a university, he should explore these opportunities early in the application process and pay particular attention to the eligibility requirements and the deadline for application.

Outside Scholarships

Ninety-five percent of the money a student receives for college will come from the institution he chooses to attend, either in terms of government or institutional aid. Because college has become so expensive, however, even with need-based and merit-based aid, college is still not affordable for many students.

Every year, thousands of organizations offer millions of dollars in outside scholarships to current and future students. While money is certainly available, the actual payoff may not be as large as you think. According to the Washington Post, only about one in ten students enrolled in a bachelor's degree program wins a private scholarship—with an average award of approximately $2,800[6].

What type of student is most likely to cash in? Well, that depends. Some scholarships are geared toward students who are most likely to succeed, meaning students who have proven themselves academically. Slightly more than half of all scholarships are won by students with a 3.5 to 4.0 grade point average, and nearly a third are awarded to students with a B average. Students with above average ACT and SAT scores are twice as likely to win scholarships than students with below average scores. Other scholarships, however, target students who best match criteria such as students from a particular demographic, with a specific interest or experience, or with exceptional artistic or athletic talent.

Finding a scholarship for which you are eligible is only the first step in the process. You also have to apply. I recommend searching for scholarships by deadline because it helps a student prioritize tasks. I also recommend that students consider bang for the buck (how much work is required to win what amount of money), the degree of interest the student has in the topic, and the student's ability (writing, photography, experiences) to win. It's easy to become obsessed with trying to find outside scholarships. After all, no one really wants to pay for higher education. I believe, however, if a student can find two or three scholarships for which he is eligible every month and make a concentrated effort to apply, he stands a much better chance of actually winning something than submitting a dozen easy, sweepstakes-type applications. Applying for outside scholarships should definitely be considered part of the college planning process; however, a student's primary focus should be demonstrating excellence in academics and extracurricular activities since those are the primary things colleges consider when determining merit scholarships—and the chance of a student getting an institutional scholarship is significantly greater than the chance of getting an outside scholarship. (Still, you should try for both. Everything helps!) While it's true that there are no guarantees of winning an outside scholarship just because you apply for one, you won't receive a penny if you never apply.

Include applying for outside scholarships as a part of the college planning process—and even a part of the pre-planning process. The reason many students don't win an outside scholarship is because they start too late, often as a junior or senior in high school. Scholarships can be awarded to much younger students as well as older ones. So, start looking well before college and don't stop searching until you're finished with your education.

Like many parts of the college planning process, applying for outside scholarships is a bit of a game, so learn the rules and play well:

1. Search for scholarships early (as young as ten years old), late (all the way through college), and often (at least once a month).
2. Choose wisely which scholarships you will apply for.
3. Stay away from scholarship applications that seem easy; e.g., submitting your contact information and writing three sentences about why you need a scholarship. This type of sweepstakes scholarship usually results in nothing more than adding your name to a lot of email junk lists.
4. Select scholarships based on your area of strength. If you have a passion for people with disabilities, compete for a scholarship that requires you to write an essay about disability inclusion. Conversely, if you have no interest in politics, don't apply for a scholarship that requires you to write a five-hundred-word essay on why your vote matters.
5. Consider bang for the buck. Don't write a two-thousand-word essay that carries a prize of only a hundred dollars. Instead, apply for a scholarship that requires a five-hundred-word essay for a five thousand-dollar award.
6. Make sure you not only feel strongly about the topic, but that you have a certain degree of expertise regarding the method of delivery as well. For example, if you've never made a film before, you can certainly enter a film contest, but your chances of winning will be fairly slim until you develop some skill in filmmaking. If you choose to enter a speech contest, make sure you practice your communication skills. If an essay is required, read it aloud and have someone proof it for errors.

7. Verify your eligibility for the scholarship. Read the fine print and follow the rules.
8. National scholarships are great, but the smaller the applicant pool, the greater the chance you have of winning. Search for scholarships that have specific eligibility, activity, or interest requirements that you fit into, for example, scholarships for New Mexicans, scholarships for children of military personnel, scholarships for musicians, community service scholarships, leadership scholarships, photography scholarships, etc. Many businesses and organizations offer scholarships specifically to children of employees and active members.
9. There are a variety of websites that offer free lists of scholarships. Fastweb.com (https://www.fastweb.com) and scholarships.com (https://www.scholarships.com) are two of my favorites. Be very hesitant if a scholarship search engine or a scholarship application requires payment. I consider this a red flag.
10. Whenever possible, search by the deadline. This will help you prioritize when to apply for what scholarships. Students can also search by a specific topic such as "scholarships for debaters" or "scholarships for New Yorkers."
11. Applying for scholarships can be quite time consuming, but it can pay off. Think of applying for scholarships (outside and institutional) as part of your job. If you are fortunate enough to win a large scholarship after writing an essay or doing a project, the award could turn into the best hourly wage you'll ever garner, e.g., winning ten thousand dollars for an essay that took five hours to write, edit, and submit equates to a salary of two thousand dollars per hour.
12. Since applying for scholarships is time-consuming, I recommend parents and students work as a team. Parents can search for scholarships initially (through websites or a topical search) and forward anything they view as a good possibility to the student. The student should apply for no more than two or three scholarships per month. Students

should spend the majority of their time demonstrating academic strength and extracurricular potential—not applying for scholarships.
13. Money from outside scholarships may be paid in cash, savings bond, or direct payment to a university. If a student wins an award prior to enrolling in college and the method of payment is the latter, most organizations provide the winner with a form that the student submits to the paying organization upon matriculation to an institution. Don't worry needlessly about this. Most organizations are very responsible regarding scholarship administration.
14. Note for Homeschoolers: Some homeschool parents search scholarship essay topics and assign appropriate topics as a school writing assignment. In this way, the essay can serve as both an educational requirement and a scholarship application.

Other Financial Considerations

Most families want to have an idea of how much a school will cost before the student applies. Unfortunately, this is becoming harder and harder to evaluate. This is why, several years ago, the United States government mandated that each university include a net price calculator (sometimes called a scholarship calculator) on its website. A student can input certain information such as his parents' income, his GPA, and his test scores, and the calculator will estimate his out-of-pocket cost. Unfortunately, many of these calculators are very general and, therefore, very inaccurate. The more specific the information required for the net price calculator, the more accurate the estimate will be.

A student can calculate his EFC/SAI which enables him to determine his potential for need-based aid (depending on the price of the school and the average percentage of need the school meets). He may also be able to estimate merit money (especially if the school has chart-based scholarships), but until a student actually receives an offer from a school, he won't know the exact out-of-pocket cost.

Because of the high cost of college, most families cannot pay for college by simply deducting payments from their income. Higher education is an investment, and thus, requires financial planning and a diligent savings plan.

Many families begin saving for college as soon as their child is born or even prior to that. The theory of compounding interest (starting to save earlier rather than later) is extraordinary and should be explored by anyone saving for college. Some parents invest in stocks or ETFs (exchange traded funds) early on, and, as the student gets older, they move the investments into safer vehicles such as CDs. Parents should educate themselves financially to make sure they understand the risks that come with particular investments. Because of the formula used to calculate need-based aid, it's always more beneficial to save under the parents' names rather than the student's name. Many families prefer using a 529 plan for such a purpose.

Recognizing the soaring cost of college, federal and state governments and many businesses have instituted tax credits or educational savings incentives. Each family should explore its options based on location, occupation, and income and tax brackets.

If a family is unable to save a significant amount of money for a student's higher education, the student can still attend college, but he would be well-advised to demonstrate his full potential throughout high school. In this way, universities will find him an attractive candidate with great potential who simply needs a chance to succeed. Thus, the university has the unique opportunity to play the benevolent fairy-godmother in a student's Cinderella-style success story—giving the institution a positive public relations image which can lead to higher rankings and more popularity, which, in turn, results in more money for the institution. (Don't kid yourself. Although most colleges are designated as non-profit institutions, they are first and foremost a business, and as such, they are in the business of filling classrooms and beds.)

A separate book could be written on paying for college, and many excellent ones have been. Educate yourself on the cost of higher education. Colleges come in a variety of prices and payment options including need-blind schools, international colleges and universities (many with three-year degrees), military academies, junior colleges, and work colleges.

In addition to the financial sacrifice a family makes, a student should also take responsibility for his education, certainly academically and, in at least some way, financially. This could be done through earning scholarships or tuition discounts, maintaining strong grades, progressing through college in order to graduate on time, saving money (if the student has income) and managing expenses wisely—both before and during college.

Additional ways to make college more affordable include having the student stick to a budget by controlling personal costs (entertainment, transportation, etc.), shortening the time required in college by the student's participation in CLEP or AP tests, dual credit courses, and summer school; having the student take general education courses online or at a less expensive university and transfer to a more specialized school during the last two years, buying used or online books, choosing less expensive dorms (or living accommodations) and dining plans, getting an on or off-campus job, applying to be a resident assistant, or serving in ROTC (letting the military pick up all or part of the bill for the student's education in exchange for several years of military service). One very popular option for students living near a university is to live at home while attending classes—either for the first two years or until graduation. While this can be cost efficient, if a family decides this is the best option, both the parents and the student need to be intentional about allowing the student to transition into adulthood and become more independent.

As mentioned previously, the money spent on higher education will probably be the second largest expenditure in a family's lifetime outside of purchasing its primary residence. In my opinion, it's well worth it, but we must be reasonable when evaluating the out-of-pocket cost. What's reasonable for one person may be too expensive for another. Don't let peer pressure direct your pocketbook; use wisdom. Yes, a university education is expensive, but it is also be a valuable investment—an investment that pays significant dividends for generations to come.

Chapter 7

This is a Test

One of the most stressful aspects of college planning is standardized testing. As an educator, I believe tests serve a critical purpose; that is, you don't know what you don't know until you take a test. The more I learn about ACT and SAT, however, the more I fail to see the benefit of these particular tests. That's not to say they don't have a purpose; they do. It's just that I don't believe the purpose is entirely beneficial.

As more and more students apply to multiple schools, standardized testing offers a way for institutions to compare applicants and become more or less selective. In my opinion, this is unfortunate for several reasons. First, a student is more than his test score. Every person is created with individual gifts and talents, and a student's abilities may not line up with the subjects on the test. It's akin to asking a fish to climb a tree. Just because the fish doesn't have the skill to climb a tree doesn't mean his skills aren't valuable.

Second, all too often, the pressure students feel to do well on standardized testing causes significant anxiety. For example, a student may call himself a bad test taker when, in reality, the student wasn't tested in his areas of knowledge. It may be true that the student didn't score well on ACT or SAT, but that doesn't mean he's doomed to do poorly on tests for the rest of his life.

Finally, standardized tests contain cultural bias. Simply the fact that the tests deal primarily with English and math indicates knowledge in those areas is more valuable. Granted, a particular level of mastery in both of those subjects is necessary for what is considered success in today's society, but there are a multitude of other areas that are just as important, but will never be seen on a standardized test: communication skills, personal responsibility, and creativity, to name a few.

The pandemic caused universities to re-evaluate the importance of SAT and ACT scores. Because so many tests were cancelled in 2020, most colleges transitioned to test-optional, at least for a season. As the world emerges from the pandemic, some colleges will remain test-optional and others will return to the testing requirement.

Because we cannot know the ultimate decisions of universities regarding their preference for SAT and ACT scores, for the time being, testing remains a critical component of the college planning process. What does it mean when a school says it is test-optional? Basically, that school does not require ACT or SAT scores as part of a student's application; however, a student may submit his test score if he feels his scores accurately represent his academic potential.

Specific rules for test optional applications vary among schools. Some colleges require an additional essay or teacher recommendation. Some universities admit without a test score, but require them for scholarship eligibility. Other institutions ask for nothing. Refer to your school's rules either on its website or on fairtest.org (http://fairtest.org), a site that offers updated information about schools offering test optional admission.

Test Types and Explanations

ACT (American College Testing) and SAT (Scholastic Assessment Test) are the primary standardized tests used for college entrance exams in the United States. While most students are familiar with these tests, sometimes confusion surrounds other undergraduate tests like PSAT/NMSQT, NHRP, CLT (Classic Learning Test), SAT II, AP Tests, CLEP (College Level Examination Program), and TOEFL (Test of English as a Foreign Language). (Graduate level exams such as GRE, LCAT, and GMAT are beyond the scope of this book.)

PSAT is probably the most well-known of the secondary tests. Designed by CollegeBoard, it serves as a "practice" SAT (hence, the "P"). Most schools offer the test to its tenth graders to discover testing potential, but, in my opinion, the real advantage of the PSAT is that it serves as the gateway to National Merit scholarships. The National Merit program (also known as NMSQT) offers a wide array of scholarships (some from universities and some from private sources) for students who score in their state's top percentile and later confirm that ability by scoring equally well on the SAT. Like SAT, PSAT evaluates a student's strength in critical reading, language, and math. I usually recommend all students take the PSAT, if possible, in tenth grade and certainly in eleventh grade, when students' scores are automatically submitted to the National Merit Scholarship Corporation. Unlike other tests that are offered year-round, PSAT is only offered in October. Because so much anxiety surrounds standardized testing and since college admission is not based on PSAT, I recommend all students take the test to become familiar with the testing process. Students should prepare for PSAT by taking one or two practice tests (usually available in a hard copy from their high school counselor or electronically online). If a student takes PSAT (or any standardized test) without studying, his score may be abnormally low which can lead to significant insecurities regarding future testing. If a student is academically inclined (4.0+ GPA), I advise additional preparation for PSAT because those students have a real chance of scoring high enough in eleventh grade to actually become a National Merit Semifinalist (NMSQT) or a National Hispanic Recognition Program (NHRP) finalist, both of which can open the door to numerous scholarships.

The CLT (Classical Learning Test) is an alternative standardized test geared for more classically taught high school students. In other words, the test focuses on western teachings by notable thinkers as opposed to the common core. Most of the forty-plus colleges that accept CLT are faith-based schools, and many of the students who take CLT are home educated.

Since SAT is theoretically a critical reasoning test, many years ago, Collegeboard created a complementary exam that assesses students' abilities in particular areas, notably foreign language, math, history, and science. Over the last decade, however, SAT II Subject Tests have diminished in popularity, and with the complications of the pandemic, Collegeboard determined it will no longer offer SAT II Subject tests after June 2021.

Advanced Placement tests (AP) offer students the opportunity to gain college credit from classes taken in high school. Students enroll in an AP level course in high school and, upon completion, take a test to determine their level of mastery. Depending on the student's score (1-5) and the student's university, a student may or may not receive college credit. Sometimes this credit manifests in terms of actual college credit; other times, it allows the student to enroll in a more advanced level of a required course.

CLEP exams allow students to test out of college-level general education courses. Different colleges accept different CLEP tests, so a student should never take a CLEP test until he knows which university he will attend and which of the thirty-three tests the university accepts. CLEP tests may be taken while a student is still in high school, the summer prior to the student attending college, or throughout the first year of college. Check your institution's rules regarding the timing of and procedures for these tests.

TOEFL is an examination for students whose native language is not English, but who wish study at an English-speaking university.

ACT versus SAT

ACT and SAT are two different tests. While there is crossover in the concepts required to succeed on both tests, the manner in which the questions are asked differs significantly. Therefore, I usually advise that a student determines which test is more appropriate for his unique learning style and start with that test.

Several decades ago, SAT was the preferred test for universities on the east and west coasts. ACT was considered the test used by middle America. That has changed. All colleges accept both ACT and SAT and show no partiality towards either test. Granted, more universities superscore SAT than ACT, but that doesn't mean the test is preferred. Superscoring means that a student can submit scores from more than one test date, and the university considers the highest score for each section regardless of the date of the test. Many times, this results in a higher average score than if only one test was considered. More and more schools are doing this for ACT as well, but because of the nature of ACT, superscoring usually doesn't result in as much of an increase.

How can a student determine which test is more appropriate for him? The most efficient way is to take a diagnostic, but students can also take all or a portion of each test (ACT and SAT), score the tests, and compare the scores on a concordance chart.

Three primary differences exist between ACT and SAT:

1. ACT is a much faster paced exam than SAT. This is because ACT asks more direct questions than SAT. SAT requires more critical reasoning skills and, therefore, gives students more time to answer questions. ACT requires a student to answer 214 questions in 175 minutes; SAT requires a student to answer 154 questions in 180 minutes.
2. ACT is completely multiple choice. SAT has a few "grid-ins" (fill-in-the-blank questions) in the math sections.
3. ACT has a separate science section. (SAT does cover science, but it is incorporated in the critical reading and language sections).

Regarding individual sections, SAT's critical reading section contains "proof of evidence" questions in which the student must locate the evidence he used to answer a previous question. SAT may utilize graphs in its critical reading section in order to test a student's ability to read graphs. ACT does not include these types of questions.

In the English section (which SAT calls language), SAT focuses more on rhetoric (how an idea is expressed) rather than the mechanics (punctuation, verb tense, etc.). The opposite is true for ACT.

ACT asks students to find straightforward answers to math questions; SAT may ask the student to choose an equation that most accurately expresses the manner in which the solution can be found. SAT math includes a no calculator section and grid-ins (fill-in-the-blank questions). SAT math includes considerably more algebra questions than geometry questions and expects students to know concepts through Algebra II; ACT includes four basic trigonometry questions and has about sixty percent algebra problems and forty percent geometry problems.

ACT's science section requires students to extrapolate information from charts, graphs, and passages in order to draw scientific conclusions. SAT does not have this section.

Both tests currently have optional essay sections. SAT's essay section asks the student to analyze another writer's argument; however, SAT will no longer offer the essay section after June 2021. ACT asks the student to form an opinion about a particular issue and compare and contrast his conclusion with other views.

Two changes are on the horizon for ACT, although at the time of this book's publication, they are not implemented. ACT is planning to allow students to re-take one section of the test at a time, beginning sometime in 2021. ACT is also hoping to fully computerize its test.

Because standardized testing requires both conceptual knowledge and test-taking skills, most students don't demonstrate their full potential until they have taken the test two or three times. After a student takes a test three times, the chances of a student raising his score diminishes; therefore, if a student prepares well and, after taking the test several times, fails to demonstrate his potential, he should consider switching tests. In my practice, I find that two-thirds of students do better on one test or the other, so I don't normally recommend students take both tests. This is, of course, a personal choice, and if a student feels he has time to adequately prepare for both tests, a student may take both.

Occasionally, a student experiences such severe test anxiety that his final scores on both tests fail to demonstrate his ability. In this case, the student should consider test optional schools.

Test Success

Test anxiety and peer pressure definitely contribute to students' anxieties about standardized testing. In reality, however, the tests are fairly simple—as long as a student knows the rules of the game. I believe, in order for a student to demonstrate his potential in standardized testing, he needs to do three things:

1. Know the concepts
2. Apply the strategies
3. Practice for confidence

Throughout high school, hopefully, students have mastered the concepts necessary for the math and English portions of ACT or SAT. If a student has a "hole" in his education, he may need to learn new theories or rules. Many websites and practice books provide thorough reviews of the concepts. My favorite resource for learning or reviewing ACT and SAT concepts is the appropriate book (SAT or ACT) from Applerouth publishing (https://www.applerouth.com/materials/). My second favorite resource is the free, online teaching at Collegeboard's Kahn Academy (https://www.khanacademy.org/).

Regarding concepts, a few things to remember are:

1. Basic concepts are most important, e.g., punctuation, subject/verb agreement, probability, quadratic equations, functions.
2. Because the tests are timed, the student needs to know the concepts well. The tests don't allow time for the student to stop and think.
3. Many times, the concepts students have the most problems with are the ones students have forgotten—not the "hardest" concepts, but the ones students haven't practiced in several years.

Knowing test strategies means knowing how to play the game. Being able to apply appropriate strategies helps in every section of testing, but it's particularly important in the critical reading (ACT/SAT) and science sections (ACT). Students have a tendency to ignore strategies when preparing for tests, but they are well worth studying. General strategies include:

1. Practicing time management
2. Controlling test anxiety
3. Knowing what the question is asking
4. Using process of elimination to find the right answer
5. Being able to solve a question more than one way
6. Recognizing standard traps in each test
7. Answering every question, even if it's a guess (points are not deducted for wrong answers)

Specific math strategies include knowing how to translate the problem, backsolving, using plug-ins, realizing questions get harder (and take longer) as the test progresses, and not getting stuck.

Effective strategies to employ in the English section are reading in context, avoiding redundancy, staying on topic, transitioning well, and letting the answer choices guide you to the error.

In critical reading, the primary strategy I recommend is process of elimination. While evidence should always exist in the reading passage, it helps to know that it's usually easier to find the wrong answers than the right one. A student should pay attention to every word in each answer choice. Many times, one word will invalidate the entire answer. Additionally, sometimes the simplest answer is the best; complicated answers are meant to confuse the reader.

ACT has a separate science section, but it's not about science. The ACT science section evaluates the student's abilities to visually extrapolate information and understand inference. Whenever possible, the student should go immediately to the question and look for key words. Many times, the student can find information relating to the key words on a chart or a graph and doesn't have to read the passage. Sometimes, the student has to read the information for an explanation or definition, but if a student reads everything in the science section, he'll never finish on time.

Once a student has mastered the concepts and the strategies for ACT and SAT, he still needs to practice. Often, I compare the necessity of practicing for standardized tests to that of practicing a sport. Even if you know all the rules and strategies, if you never practice, you won't do very well. The same thing is true for ACT and SAT. Practice also reduces test anxiety. The more familiar the student is with the tricks of the test, the more confident he'll become.

Many of the calls I receive from students asking for help with standardized testing start with, "I took it once without preparation, and scored X." In my opinion, taking a test without preparation is a waste of time and money. Why risk having a low score when a low score can be such a psychological block?

Initially, a student should prepare approximately fifty to sixty hours over a period of ten to twelve weeks for his first standardized test. Students are absolutely capable of preparing for standardized testing by themselves if they purchase a book and carefully work through it, but many students find that using a personal coach or attending a test prep class offers accountability and provides a more efficient, structured way of preparing for the test. Test prep is not cheap, but it can be highly beneficial because so many schools consider test scores when giving scholarships.

Because of the overall college application timeline and the nature of ACT and SAT, students should consider taking ACT or SAT as soon as they've completed Algebra I, Geometry, and Algebra II. This could be as early as the sophomore year. Most students wait until the junior year to take the tests, but in my opinion, if a student is familiar with the necessary math concepts, he should go ahead and take the test. Waiting only serves to delay the inevitable, causing more anxiety and more stress. And there's enough of that already.

CHAPTER 8

SPECIAL CIRCUMSTANCES

The typical college application is not difficult; it's just time-consuming. In certain circumstances, however, supplemental information is needed because additional factors play into a student's acceptance. In those cases, the student must devote extra time to the application process to meet the additional requirements.

Arts Programs

Acceptance into some university-level fine arts programs (theatre, music, film, visual arts) requires either an audition or a portfolio. The college may offer students options such as recorded, live, or off-campus auditions on several days, or it may be less flexible. Guidelines are usually posted on the university's website, but if the student has any questions, the student should contact either the department or the admissions office. In any case, the student should carefully study the requirements and make sure he adheres to them. Sometimes deadlines for departmental applications are earlier than the university's general deadline for admission, and sometimes they are later. It is possible for a student to be accepted to an institution but denied admission to a particular program. In such cases, the student will need to decide how important admission to a particular department is as opposed to the university as a whole.

Honors College

Some students want the individual attention of a small school, but the feeling of a large university. These students usually find exactly what they need in an honors college (or honors program) at a large university. (In this case, a college is similar to a department at a university.) Most honors-level courses at universities are not necessarily harder; instead, they are more discussion-based and have additional academic or research opportunities. If a student finds the academic environment of the honors college too rigorous, a student can usually change to the traditional track fairly easily. Admission requirements for honors colleges vary: some are by invitation only (based on test scores and high school GPA); some require separate essays or recommendations; some don't accept freshmen until second semester. Acceptance to an honors college can be more challenging than admission to the university itself. Sometimes a student is admitted to the university, but not the honors college. At that point, the student has to determine how important admission to the honors college is versus admission to the university.

Direct-entry Majors

Most students do not officially declare their major at a university until the end of their sophomore year. Nevertheless, most freshmen already have an idea of what they want to study. Sometimes, when a university is unable to accommodate all the students who want to major in a particular field (usually due to a lack of facilities or faculty), the major becomes impacted. Students then must compete for the opportunity to major in that area. Many times, the determining factor for admission to the major is student's prior academic record. Sometimes, additional tests or recommendations are used. If a student isn't accepted into his major, he is usually welcome to apply again later, but there is never a guarantee he will be admitted.

In contrast, other schools offer direct-entry majors. This means there are no additional competitive requirements to gain entry to any field of study. Granted, admission to the major may require particular grades in certain prerequisite classes, but the student will not find himself denied entry to a major due to competition among students.

Athletic Recruiting

When a student wants to play NCAA sports, the process of college admissions becomes much more intense. In order for a student to be considered, he must be both an outstanding athlete and an above-average student. Every student who is interested in being recruited must register with the NCAA Clearing House and must meet certain academic requirements to be eligible for recruitment. If a student is interested in playing college sports, he should ask for an honest assessment from his high school coach. The student and his family should become familiar with the recruiting process and learn how to catch the attention of a college coach. Since the process of recruiting varies according to the sport, each student athlete should research his particular sport and determine the best methods of recruitment.

GED

Some students are unable to complete high school due to special circumstances (chronic illness, olympic competitions, professional acting jobs, etc.) Students can still receive a high school diploma and, in many cases, be accepted to college after passing a comprehensive test called a GED. Specific requirements are available from each state's department of higher education.

Homeschool Notes

Before I get into the nitty gritty of actual applications, I need to share a few thoughts about home education. I home educated for twenty years, and my children were incredibly successful in college. They both received full ride scholarships and graduated with top honors. Home education works—but it's not for everyone.

Many families home educate during primary and middle school, but are concerned about homeschooling in high school because of the college application process. They fear universities will not look favorably on homeschooled students.

While this may be true in some circumstances, most universities realize home educated students are intelligent and engaged. Most colleges accept a home school diploma as proof of high school graduation, although a few schools require homeschooled students to earn a GED (General Education Diploma) to be eligible for admission or scholarships. In order to receive a GED, a student must pass a general education test near the end of his high school career. (See earlier section in this chapter.)

On a personal level, I've witnessed the extremes of colleges' views on homeschooling. When my younger daughter had an interview with an Ivy League school, the first thing the interviewer said to her was, "I love homeschooled students. They know how to learn!"

My older daughter received a different response in a similar situation when the interviewer asked her, "What's it like to go to school in your pajamas?"

Tactfully, my daughter replied, "I don't know. I've never been to school in my pajamas."

When a family decides to homeschool through high school, the entire family needs to make education a top priority. The parent needs to make sure the student has plenty of opportunities to challenge himself through activities such as cooperative teaching, college-level classes, extracurricular pursuits, internships, and competitions.

From the very beginning, the parent should keep track of educational endeavors by creating a graded transcript, a description of classes, and an activities resumé. Templates for all these documents can be found online or in the appendix of this book. Each document needs to be updated regularly in order to demonstrate the depth and breadth of the student's high school education.

When a homeschooled student applies to college, he needs to (like all applicants) submit a transcript. The transcript consists of a year-by-year listing of all high school and college prep classes with appropriate grades and credits, including classes taken outside the home, e.g., dual credit courses, junior college classes, online learning, and traditional high school courses. The homeschool parent submits the transcript in a separate envelope with a cover letter, and the envelope should be sealed with the parent's signature over the seal. If a homeschooled, high school student has taken classes at an accredited institution (college, junior college, online high school, or traditional high school), the student should also ask the accredited institutions to submit an official transcript to each school where he is applying. Fewer and fewer colleges require course descriptions as a required component for home educated students, but some still do. Therefore, the parent should have this information available in case it is requested.

As part of the college application process, a homeschooler may be asked for a teacher or counselor recommendation. Parents are usually not allowed to complete these forms. If the student has taken advantage of outside educational opportunities as mentioned above, the student should be able to get a recommendation from a mentor or outside teacher.

Home education gives students the necessary skills to succeed in college. Because of the nature of home education, most homeschoolers are extremely self-motivated. They've discovered how to make the most of their particular learning style. Homeschoolers are also self-directed. They recognize their areas of interest and have often had real-world, experiential opportunities. Successful homeschoolers have also learned the value of teamwork through extracurricular and service activities.

When well-implemented, homeschooling provides effective education for students. Colleges and universities recognize the benefits that come with personalized education and welcome homeschooled students to further their education and get the tools they need for adulthood.

Chapter 9

Applying to College

Overview

Life was simpler when your parents applied to college, and many adults are baffled by how much the process has changed. But it has. Applying to college is a multi-step, competitive process, and if a student wants to get accepted and gain some merit-based money, he has to do what's required.

Officially, the college application season opens August 1st of the student's senior year although, in an effort to compete for students, some universities make their online applications available earlier. Applying to college is a process that's often filled with stress, but it is my hope that after reading this book, you'll be able to negotiate the process more easily.

The National Candidate Reply Deadline for all American colleges is May 1st. This means that if a school offers a student admission, the institution must save a place for the student as long as the student replies by May 1st of the student's senior year. (Read more about this in chapter ten.)

The requirements for a college application vary considerably (depending on the institution and the major), but the most common elements are:

1. Application (Some applications are specific to the school; other institutions utilize what I call a collaborative application, when one application that can be used as an application for multiple schools. Collaborative applications include the Common Application, the Universal Application,

the Coalition Application, Apply Texas, the University of California application, and several others.)
2. Activities resumé (This may be included as part of the application, or the student may be asked to submit a separate resumé. See a sample format in appendix.)
3. Main Essay (Sometimes more than one essay is required. See below.)
4. Counselor recommendation (This frequently includes a school report which gives context to the student's education.)
5. Teacher recommendation (Even if a teacher recommendation is optional, I highly suggest submitting one if the university allows it.)
6. Official school transcript (Requested by the student, sent directly from the high school to the university. A student should ensure all grades, including dual credit courses, summer school classes, and school transfers are on the official transcript.)
7. Official ACT and/or SAT test scores (Requested by the student, sent directly from the testing agency. Not required by test-optional or test-blind schools.)

Additional components may include:

1. AP or IB test scores (Many times, these are optional and self-reported until the student decides to matriculate.)
2. Creative portfolio or audition (Frequently required for creative arts majors or students seeking a BFA degree. If a student does plan on majoring in a creative field, he should definitely check the school's website for information regarding deadlines and requirements.)
3. Supplemental essays (Topics can run the gamut from a single question such as "Why do want to attend this school" to seven or eight questions dealing with such topics as "How do plan to be the change you want to see?" or "Name your top ten.")

4. Interview (Many times, the interview is optional for admission, but required for acceptance to special programs such as a BSMD (an accelerated program to medical school) or top scholarships. An interview may be with an admissions representative, a current student, or an alumnus.)
5. FAFSA (This form must be completed in order to be eligible for need-based aid. See chapter six.)
6. CSS Profile (Required by about 200 institutions in order to be eligible for institutional financial aid. See chapter six.)
7. Scholarship application (While most scholarship applications are automatic, some top scholarships require additional applications, essays, or recommendations. Check the school's website.)
8. Honors college application (Honors college applications vary widely. Some are by invitation; some are by application; some require an essay, and some don't. You can apply anytime at some schools and only after general acceptance at other schools.)

Ideally, by the end of a student's junior year, the student should have his college list. Once he has his list, a student should go online and look at the various application requirements and deadlines for each school. Based on that research, the student should create an overall application schedule.

Most schools have several types of deadlines. Regular decision (RD) is, as the name implies, the standard deadline. This date can vary widely, from October to the following June. If a student is really interested in a school, however, the student should demonstrate his interest by applying early. There are three types of "early deadlines":

Early Action (EA): For most schools, the deadline for early action is November 1st, however some schools have their EA deadline in December. The benefit of applying early action is that the university notifies the student more quickly about acceptance and usually about scholarships (generally by February 1st). An early action acceptance is non-binding, meaning a student can apply to as many schools as he wants EA and RD, compare his offers of admittance and financial aid and make his decision regarding where he will attend as late as May 1st.

Restrictive Early Action (REA): If a student applies REA and the student is accepted, the student is not obligated to accept the offer of admission (just like in early action). However, if a student applies restrictive early action, the student agrees to not apply to any other school in the early rounds. In other words, by applying REA, the student is indicating that school is a top choice, but the family is not willing to commit financially until the offer of financial aid and scholarships occurs.

Early Decision (ED): A student should only apply early decision if the university is absolutely the student's first choice and if the family agrees to pay up to the full price of the school. When a student applies early decision, the student agrees to apply to only one school early decision. Usually (but not always), the student can apply to other schools early action, but not restrictive early action. A student can apply to other institutions through regular decision, but if the student is accepted to a college ED, the student must immediately withdraw all other college applications. The university that accepts the student ED is under no obligation to guarantee any particular amount of financial aid, although many schools that offer early decision plans provide generous need-based aid. When the student receives notification of scholarships and financial aid from the ED school (usually considerably later than the notification of acceptance), if the family can justify the fact that it truly cannot afford the school, the family can explain the situation, and the college will usually release the student. By this time, however, many other schools' deadlines have passed. Acceptance rates in the early decision pool are often higher than in the regular decision pool; therefore, a student may have a better chance of acceptance by applying early decision. Bear in mind, however, if a student is accepted early decision, he is committed to attending that university regardless of the expense.

Getting a Jump on Applications

Because of the various components of the college application and the overall busyness of students once school starts, I recommend getting a jump on college applications during the summer between the junior and senior years. This can make a huge difference in the stress level during the application process.

During the summer before a student's senior year, he should:

1. Make final visits to universities if necessary. (This might happen if the student has been unable to visit the school while it was in session. Alternatively, a student may choose to visit a college during the early fall of his senior year, although this can be difficult to schedule with all the obligations of the senior year.)
2. Take a final round of standardized tests if necessary.
3. Use the summer to demonstrate his potential (and his tag, described in chapter four) through activities, shadowing, and service projects, and update his resumé (see information below) to reflect his endeavors.
4. Apply for scholarships or search for scholarships to apply for later in the year.
5. Finalize the college list.
6. Preview all requirements necessary for admission to each university including deadlines, essays, letters of recommendation, scholarships, honors college applications, and major-specific additional materials. This is done by looking at a school's website.
7. If you do plan to apply via the Common Application, Universal Application, or Coalition Application, complete as much of the application as possible during the summer and write the main essay. The general applications, although tedious, are fairly easy. The Common Application, Universal Application, and Coalition Application always release their essay topics in the spring, but themes for supplemental essays and school-specific essays tend to change from year to year. Therefore, I recommend working only on the main

essay for those collaborative applications during the summer—not the school-specific, supplemental essays. (See below for more information regarding essay writing tips.) Note: Don't panic when the collaborative application sites go dark several days in July in order to update; your information will be saved.

8. Based on each school's requirements and deadlines and where the school ranks in your list (favorite schools should be a priority), create a list of all the elements required to apply to each school (including special programs and scholarships) and an overall timeline. Application requirements are usually available on the undergraduate "how to apply" page of each university's website. In addition to finding out what is required in order to apply to the institution, a student should also see if additional items are needed to apply to a specific major, honors college, or special scholarship. If you have questions regarding the timing or the details of a school's application process (such as auditions, interviews, self-reported grades or scores, etc.), call the university's office of admissions. The timeline should be driven by the application deadlines and how high the school is on the student's list. A student should always plan to submit his application at least one week before the deadline. Life gets busy, and even the most well-organized student needs a little flexibility in case he gets delayed. See the appendix for a sample of a Requirements Document and an Application Timeline.

The Resumé: Who Are You?

An activities resumé is an important part of a student's college application. But it's not only important for the application; it also plays a role when a student applies for membership in an organization or seeks a job. Numerous resumé templates are available online, but I've also included a very simple template in the appendix of this book.

Several things make the resumé for college applications unique:

1. List activities by category (academic, athletics, fine arts, leadership, service, etc.) with the most important category first. (The most important category is usually the category that is most relevant to what the student will be studying or most indicative of his tag.) For example, if a student wants to be a business major, he should probably list his leadership accomplishments or employment experiences first. If a student is applying to be an art major, artistic endeavors should be at the top of the resumé.
2. Within each category, list the most important accomplishments first. Activities and accomplishments do not need to be listed chronologically.
3. Only list items that the student pursued after first semester of ninth grade. For example, if a student began playing soccer in second grade, but stopped playing soccer in eighth grade, it should not be included on his college resumé. If he continued playing soccer throughout ninth grade, it could go on the resumé with the second-grade year as the starting date.
4. List the start date and the end date. If the student is still continuing the activity when he submits the resumé, the end date should say "present."
5. List the position name and the name of the organization. Describe the position in terms of tangible accomplishments, awards, etc. Limit the description to two or three lines.
6. If at all possible, keep the resumé to one page.
7. You may be able to upload the resumé as part of the college application, or you may need to copy the information on the resumé to an application form.
8. Start the resumé early (freshman year) and continue to update it.

The College Essay: Getting the Inside Out

One of the primary hurdles most students have in the college application process is the dreaded college essay. In order to try to allay students' fears, a few years ago, most universities began calling this section a personal statement. After all, that's what it really is: a story about the student that demonstrates a particular aspect (a tag-see chapter four) or characteristic of the student's life.

Many main essay prompts are extremely broad, such as "describe an experience that changed your life" or "tell us about someone who has impacted you." Some applications simply state, "Tell us your story." Choose a topic that ties into your tag (see chapter four) and one you enjoy writing about, a story that's important to you. It could be a theme that runs through your life or a single event that demonstrates problem-solving, decision-making, creativity, or persistence. Many times, one essay will suffice for several prompts, so if you plan ahead (by assessing the requirements needed for every application), you can save time.

If you're really struggling for ideas, check out "College Essay Guy" website (https://www.collegeessayguy.com/). In my opinion, Ethan Sawyer, the "college essay guy," is one of the best in the business. He offers tons of free advice that will get you on the right track.

The most common problem students have with writing the college essay, however, doesn't require professional advice to remedy it. It requires writing...because the main problem most students have is writer's block. To overcome writer's block, a person has to write. You can't just think about it. You have to get something down on paper. If this is difficult for you, try recording your story and transcribing it. You may start a story and decide it isn't right. That's fine. Start again; try something else. Don't judge yourself too harshly. When you write the first draft, focus on the content, not the technique. Just get the story out.

The important thing to remember about writing the personal statement is that you're the expert. Never write about what you think the admission representative wants to hear; just write about you.

Think of the essay prompt as the frame of a picture—a starting point. The picture must be YOU, the student. If you write about an experience or a person who had an influence on you, don't focus on the what; focus on the who—you. In fact, the essay should be so specific that if you dropped a copy in the hallway of your school and a friend found it, that person would know the essay is yours—even if it didn't have your name on it.

Write your personal statement in such a way that the admissions representative is forced to read it. Start with a hook, not a thesis. Don't give the story away at the very beginning. Let the reader walk through the experience with you. If possible, when you close the essay, relate it back to the beginning. You don't have to share a moral of the story at the end. If the story is well-written, admissions representatives will understand the insight you gained. You don't have to explain it.

A few more tips:

1. Your reactions to an event often tell us more than your actions.
2. A simple, every-day example is often most effective. Stories about "big moments" tend to sound cliché.
3. Keep the story small, personal, and genuine.
4. Include sensory details. Let the reader experience the story with you.
5. Dialogue is powerful. People love to eavesdrop.
6. Pay attention to the word or character count.
7. Be selective regarding who edits your essay. Make sure the statement stays in the student's voice.

After you've written your first draft, set it aside for a day. Then, go back and adjust the mechanics (punctuation, phrasing, vocabulary, etc.) Read it aloud or have someone you respect read it aloud to you. What do you discover about the writer? Can you identify a few of his core values? Is the writer genuine? Is the essay well-crafted? Edit your story again, and set it aside for a couple of days. Repeat the process until you're satisfied with your essay. Ideally, you won't spend weeks writing it. Once you decide on your story, it shouldn't take more than three or four revisions to get the main essay where you want it.

What about those smaller supplemental essays? Remember, these topics often change from year to year so don't start the supplemental essay until you're sure it's the right prompt. Many students make the mistake of thinking the supplemental essays aren't important. The opposite is true. For schools that participate in a collaborative application, the individual essay is critical, especially the question that asks, "Why do you want to attend this school?"

Remember, the goal of every essay is to get to know the person behind the paper, the student behind the statistics. If you have to write about what major you prefer or why you want to attend a particular school, just like in the main essay, the spotlight should be on you. Don't write about what a wonderful school it is; the admissions representative knows that already. Write about what you're looking for in a university and why that institution satisfies those needs. Don't write about how exciting a particular field of study is; write about what you want to do in that area and how the school will help you do that.

Getting a jump on the college essay as well as the other aspects of the college application during the summer before a student's senior year will significantly minimize the stress once application season opens (on or around August 1st). Working ahead can be one of the most beneficial things you can do to ensure a successful college application process.

Going Live

The primary challenge for most students in the throes of the college application process is to continue doing well in school while still demonstrating leadership and initiative in extracurricular activities AND finding the time and energy to complete college applications effectively and on time. Once college applications go live, in order to meet most deadlines, the student should expect to spend a minimum of six hours per week on college applications until his applications are complete. If a student has a fairly long list (more than eight schools) or a complicated application process (with supplemental applications or applications for honors colleges and scholarships), the student can expect to spend even more time.

When your school applications go live, if you haven't done so already, establish an application account for each school. You may have already done this for your collaborative applications. For applications such as the Common App, the Coalition App, Apply Texas, or the University of California system, you need to choose (add) the names of the schools to which you want to apply. Some collaborative applications require the student to apply to one school at a time then copy the application for additional schools. Other systems allow the student to apply to multiple schools at one time.

After the student has established an account for each application, the student should proceed with the application process as planned earlier. A student should submit a school's application at least one week prior to its deadline in case the student falls behind.

In order to ease into the process, I usually recommend a student work on an application first. Filling in facts is easy, and progress on an application gives a sense of accomplishment. Collaborative applications such as The Common Application, the Coalition Application, and Apply Texas are tedious and require extra time, so they're a good place to start. (Just get it over with!) Some of the requested information (class size, class rank, cumulative GPA) may only be available from the student's counselor, so as soon as school starts, the student should get that information from his counselor. If a student updated his resumé during the summer, completing the activities list on the application is a simple matter of copying information from his resumé to his application. If a student completed his main essay during the summer, he should proof it again, confirm that it still represents him well, and paste the essay into the application(s).

Recommendations

During the second or third week of school, the student should request his recommendations from his teacher(s) and/or counselor. I suggest the student create a request to each teacher or counselor and list the names of the schools, the deadline, and the method by which the recommendation will be submitted, e.g., a hard copy letter, the Common Application, an emailed form, etc. The student should attach an updated resumé to that written request and, if a hard copy is required, a stamped, addressed envelope. If possible, the student should meet with the potential recommender to verbally request the recommendation. If that person agrees to write the recommendation, the student should give the written request to the recommender and, because most applications ask for the recommender's contact information, the student should ask the recommender's preferred email.

A student should request recommendations early in the application process. Teachers and counselors are busy and need time to compose a strong recommendation. Letters of recommendation are expected to be submitted by each school's application deadline. At the same time, admissions representatives know students can only control the timing of the recommendation request, not the submission. Most universities allow students to track the application process on their student account. Therefore, if the deadline is approaching and the student sees the recommender has not yet submitted his recommendation, he should approach the recommender tactfully and say, "I noticed you haven't had the opportunity to complete my letter of recommendation for college. Do you need any additional information from me?"

Usually, the recommender won't need anything except for a gentle reminder. After you see he has submitted the letter of recommendation, hand write a thank you note and let him know you appreciate his assistance.

Requesting Transcripts and Scores

In early September, the student should request his official transcript be sent to each school to which he is applying. An official transcript means the transcript comes directly from the school. Every high school's process for requesting transcripts varies. Some high schools use an electronic system such as Parchments, Naviance, SCOIR, or the Common Application. At other schools, students request official transcripts through their counselor or a registrar. Usually, the student requests his transcripts by submitting a form with a list of school names and, sometimes, the address of each school, which can easily be found on the school's website. A few institutions allow students to self-report grades and don't require the submission of official transcripts until the student matriculates to the school. This information is available on the university's website. If a student has attended more than one high school, the student should verify that all his grades are included on his transcript. If a student has completed any dual credit or college-level courses, the student should request official transcripts from the college or community college as well. As mentioned previously, in the case of homeschoolers, the homeschool transcript should have all grades on it, but grades from any accredited institution (online, public school, community college) need to be verified by sending official transcripts from those schools as well.

Around the same time, the student should request his official ACT and/or SAT scores be sent to each school on his list (as desired). To do this, a student should contact either act.org or collegeboard.org, request his test scores, and pay the appropriate fee. Some schools allow a student to self-report test scores on his application and don't require receipt of official scores until the student matriculates to the institution. (Note: If you apply for honors colleges or scholarships, verify this is the proper procedure in all cases.)

Most colleges allow the student to choose which scores he wants to submit. If a school super-scores test results (uses top scores from multiple test dates on either ACT or SAT to create a higher average score), the student can send multiple test scores to each school. (Note: Schools will not "mix" scores from SAT and ACT. Select the test that better demonstrates your academic potential.) If you plan on taking additional standardized tests after you apply, you can wait to submit your test scores until after you've taken all your tests, but make sure you request those scores in plenty of time to meet the deadline. Occasionally, a school will allow a student to continue taking tests after December to qualify for higher scholarships, but generally speaking, December of the student's senior year is the last test date most schools will accept for admission consideration.

Staying on Time

The student should continue working through the application process according to his timeline: writing essays and completing applications. Students should verify whether supplemental items are required and if so, the student should complete them in a timely manner.

After the student submits his college applications, he may still need to apply to honors programs or honors colleges and scholarships. These deadlines should be on his timeline as well.

Applying to colleges requires diligence and persistence by the student. However, the reward is well worth it. If a student applies by the early action deadline (usually November 1st), he should receive notification by mid-February of both of an offer of admission and money. If a student applies to a school with a rolling deadline, he will usually hear from the institution within six weeks. If a student applies regular decision, the student may not hear from the university until the end of March.

The sooner a student finishes the application process, the sooner he'll know his options for college. Much of the stress surrounding college admissions centers on not knowing. When a student completes his applications in a timely manner, some of that anxiety will diminish, and then the student can move on to the decision process.

Chapter 10

Decisions, Decisions...

Once a student has heard from all his schools, it's time for him (with his family's assistance) to weigh his options. Some families create a spreadsheet in order to compare opportunities, costs, environment, and facts such as size or graduation rate. Some students decide to visit their top choices one more time, usually on an "accepted students' day." Some students weight certain criteria and give each school a score. Other students base the decision on a feeling. Whatever methodology you choose, I encourage you to remember, "It's not about finding a great school. It's about finding a great fit."

Financial Appeals

One of the major components in determining what school the student will attend is cost. If a student is accepted to his first-choice college, but the price is unaffordable, the student can appeal his financial aid/scholarship award.

No one wants to pay for college, but college costs. A student should not approach the appeal process with an attitude of entitlement. On the other hand, if the cost of the university is truly out of reach for the family, the student can call his admissions representative at the school and ask if there is anything he (the student) can do to make the school more affordable, e.g., apply for additional scholarships, get more grants, etc. Usually this is most effectively done in March, after an admissions representative has some idea of the matriculation rate.

Often, the admissions representative will try to determine if there has been a change in the family's financial situation since the prior-prior year of the FAFSA information. If a family has encountered a catastrophic financial event such as a death, divorce, unemployment, or chronic illness, the admissions representative may ask for documentation regarding the financial change and may reconsider the student's financial award. Occasionally, the admissions representative will evaluate the university's matriculation rate in order to determine if the school can award extra merit money to the student to seal the deal. Remember, colleges are in the business of education, and often, a school would rather give a student three thousand more dollars per year to secure a student's enrollment rather than risk the student attending another university.

Sometimes the cost difference among schools is so minor, the comparison doesn't matter. Occasionally, if everything else is equal, getting a little more money from one institution will sway the student's decision to attend the more generous university; other times, it will not.

Either way, the student and his family should agree about what school the student will attend, and once they do, student should let the college know.

Decision Time

Legally, a student has until May 1st of his senior year to make his decision regarding which college he will attend. Some colleges try to entice students to make a decision earlier, usually by offering a small scholarship to students who reply by a certain date. Remember, this is an important decision. Don't be rushed, and don't succumb to the financial pressure by replying before you're ready to.

Ultimately, a student should only deposit (reply affirmatively) to one school. Depositing at more than one school is considered unethical.

Once a student makes his decision, he should reply to the school of his choice, submit his tuition and housing deposit, and register for orientation. He should also respond to the other institutions which accepted him, thank them for their offer of acceptance, and tell them he has decided to accept another school's offer. Whew! It's a big decision, but once it's made, the stress of all the previous months of work morphs into genuine excitement.

Chapter 11

Is That All There Is?

At the risk of sounding like an infomercial, in response to the question in the title of this chapter, I have to say, "But wait...there's more." In fact, entire books have been written on the transition process from high school to college because it is such a huge transition—for both the student and the family.

Although the actual transition to college is outside the scope of this book, there are certain responsibilities that are considered "pre-transition" tasks. Yes, even after a student decides which college to attend, the college planning process still isn't over. More decisions must be made, and you have to learn to navigate "the paperwork zone."

1. If you haven't already done so, investigate the living accommodations. Most dorms have their own personality. Some have living and learning communities that house students with similar interests. Your university may ask you to fill in a questionnaire regarding roommate preferences. This is for your benefit, so do it. Some colleges will also ask you to choose your meal plan. Investigate your options and opportunities.
2. If you have not done so, get a school ID. Usually that's done when you confirm your admission decision, so memorize that number!
3. Register for freshman orientation. A few schools have separate orientation and registration procedures, but most schools offer registration during orientation. Due to class availability, it's usually better to attend registration and orientation sooner rather than later, however if your school

is far from where you live, it may be more cost effective to register during the last orientation period and simply stay at your college.
4. Before you attend orientation, sit down with the list of required general education classes and your major (if you have decided on your major and if not, classes you would like to explore) and figure out several academic schedules for the next four years. Poor planning often results in additional semesters. At the same time, be flexible. You may not get every course you want every semester.
5. If it is offered during registration, I highly recommend you meet with a college advisor to help you choose your classes and determine your schedule. Additionally, you can check with upperclassmen who help with orientation and get their suggestions on classes, professors, etc. You can also check https://www.ratemyprofessors.com/ to explore the teaching staff.
6. To be considered a full-time student, most colleges require you take a minimum of twelve credit hours. (Some scholarships may require the student to enroll in at least fifteen hours.)
7. Most schools have a parent orientation in conjunction with student orientation. I highly recommend parents take advantage of this opportunity.
8. If your school has a freshman social media page, join it.
9. Don't fret too much about your future roommate. Sometimes, you can meet someone on the social media page, or many times, you might meet someone at orientation (a possible reason to go early). Remember, when you go to college, you're in the same boat as every other freshman. They all want new friends. Put yourself out there and be willing to make new friends. You may end up having to take pot luck, but schools are usually very good at matching roommate preferences. When school starts, don't be afraid to sit with a stranger in the dining hall; keep your door some time; participate in study groups. Put yourself out there, and stick to your values. You will find your tribe.

10. Take advantage of anything your university offers specifically for freshmen, e.g., seminars, special classes, etc. You're paying for it. You might as well take advantage of it. This is your life. Make the most of it. Attend activities fairs. Get involved! If you think you might be interested, try it.
11. If you feel you need academic assistance, make sure you check out the tutoring, writing, and study skills center your school has.
12. If you're interested in the honors program, check that out. Apply.
13. Spend some time perusing your institution's website. What extracurriculars interest you? Do you want to study abroad? Do you want to be involved in Greek life or student government? Do you want to work on campus? Think about these questions and figure out how they work into your flexible four-year plan. Talk to your parents and other students about this. Find the balance between focus and exploration.
14. Write thank-you notes to all those teachers who have helped you be successful (and possibly write a note to your parents—it will mean more than you know).
15. Make sure your counselor knows where you will attend. Your counselor must send in a final transcript with the graduation date on it.
16. Check with your college and high school or community college registrar about transferring any credit for dual credit and AP classes onto your freshman transcript and how that will affect your general education requirements.
17. Decide if you want to take CLEP tests this spring or summer to get some credits out of the way. Always prepare appropriately and check with your college advisor about which CLEP tests are accepted at your institution. (This varies widely.)
18. Talk to your parents about health insurance and decide if you need the school's health insurance. You should definitely sign all HIPPA forms to make sure your parents have access to your medical records. (Your parents will know what this means.)

19. If you will not be eighteen by the time school starts, you may need to sign some additional forms for the school.
20. When you start school (or before), open your own bank account. Talk to your parents about finances and budgeting. You may also want to get a credit card, but discuss this with your parents. Be aware that your parents are spending thousands of dollars for your college education. Do your part by being responsible with your finances.
21. Talk to your parents about their expectations of you at college. Remember, if you weren't going to college, you would be working. Therefore, a rule of thumb might be to spend at least forty hours each week in class and/or studying. College is your job.
22. Decide whether you will take a car to college. Decide if you will take a computer and/or printer to college or if you need a new one. Will your cell phone plan be ok at college?
23. You may not know right now, but you and your parents may want to discuss possible summer plans (internships, etc.) as well as spring break and other holiday plans. Usually, if you're not close enough to come home for a holiday, a friend will invite you.
24. Be nice to your parents during these last months at home. They are stressed ALMOST as much as you are. Your family is making a huge sacrifice sending you to college, so be grateful. Talk about how often you plan to communicate with them when you get to school. What are their expectations? (At the same time, make sure they know that this is your time to learn how to be independent.)
25. If you lack any life skills (laundry, shopping, balancing a check book, etc.) or time management/decision-making skills, work on them!
26. Think about what items you want to take to college: clothes, books, personal items. You may want to google "packing list for college" and see what others suggest. Be careful; don't overpack.
27. Choose your priorities in college. It's easy to get distracted. Be intentional with your time and your purpose.

28. Continue searching for scholarship opportunities throughout college. Visit your financial aid and scholarship office and let them know that you are looking for additional scholarships (if indeed you are). Do this within the first two to three weeks of college.
29. If you (or your parents) have taken out a loan for college or have other special financial circumstances (VA payments, disability payments, etc.) make sure you have jumped through all the hoops. Never assume that things will take care of themselves. Call the college and ask if you aren't sure. Make certain that you know how and when you need to start repaying any loans as well as the interest rate. Federal Direct Loans (student loans) have a variety of repayment options. If a relative or friend wants to help you with your college costs, they can pay off loans for you. That way, the income doesn't count against you on next year's FAFSA.
30. Take advantage of the opportunities at college. There are soooo many! But manage your time too. Get involved!!
31. Think about what you need spiritually at college. Participate in on-campus faith groups, but also find a local church home. It's really great to be a part of an off-campus community who can support you.
32. You'll be making many new friends, but don't forget your family and friends at home. How will you stay in touch?
33. During the first two weeks of school, visit all your professors during office hours. Talk about the syllabus and their expectations and talk about yourself. Ask about opportunities. Share your dreams and expectations. If you are in a class larger than twenty students, sit in the first three rows.
34. During your four years of college, go to class. Study. Don't procrastinate. Prioritize. This is not brain surgery; it's college. Follow a few simple rules, and you will succeed.

A Request and a Special Offer

If you have found this book helpful, please PASS THE WORD. College planning should be a time of anticipation rather than anxiety. If the information you've garnered from this book has helped you, please let others know.

Additionally, if you could take a moment to do a QUICK REVIEW online, I'd be most appreciative. If you publish a review of this book online and contact me via my website (glendadurano.com) or my social media, I'll contact you and answer any specific questions YOU have about the college application process. Just be sure to write "book review" in the subject line and include your contact information in the correspondence.

Thank you for reading this book, and thank you for allowing me to serve you.

APPENDIX

Sample Resume

YOUR NAME

PHONE NUMBER　　　　　　　　　　　　　　　　　　STREET ADDRESS
EMAIL　　　　　　　　　　　　　　　　　　　　　　CITY, STATE, ZIP

LEADERSHIP

Mo/yr-Mo/yr　　*Position, Organization*
　　　　　　　　Describe what the position entailed
Mo/yr-Mo/yr　　*Position, Organization*
　　　　　　　　Try to include tangible accomplishments and results

ACADEMIC

Yr　　　　　　*Award name*
　　　　　　　　Brief description of award
Yr　　　　　　*Award name*
　　　　　　　　Awards should be listed in order of importance

COMMUNITY SERVICE

Mo/yr-Mo/yr　　*Position, Organization*
　　　　　　　　Description of service, using "power" words.
Mo/yr-Mo/yr　　*Position, Organization*
　　　　　　　　Sometimes, due to space limitations you may need to list
　　　　　　　　similar activities as one thing

CHOOSE A CATEGORY

Mo/yr-Mo/yr　　If a student has excelled in a particular category, sometimes
　　　　　　　　it is beneficial to list those achievements together, e.g.,
　　　　　　　　fine arts, sports, communication, organizations, etc.

WORK-RELATED

Mo/yr-Mo/yr　　*Position, Organization*
　　　　　　　　Work experience shows responsibility and initiative

EDUCATION

Name of School　*(GPA) (Expected Date of Graduation)*

ADDITIONAL INTERESTS

Some students wish to place interesting hobbies or travel experiences in this section. These can be individual, organizational, or familial.

Sample College Visit Form

College Advising and Planning
Campus Chronicle

School Name:_____   Address:_____
Admissions Officer:_____
Admissions Office Location:_____   Email:_____
Visit Date:_____   Phone:_____
Tour Time:_____   Interview Time:_____
Other Appointments:_____

Pre-Planning Checklist (as needed)

Transportation Plans:_____
Driving Directions/Parking Pass:_____
Overnight Housing Plans:_____
University Researched?_____ Questions to Ask?_____ Practiced Answers?_____
Appointments (as needed): (Mark "M" for "made" and "C" for "confirmed")
Tour_____ Information Session_____ Admissions Interview_____
Class Visit_____
Professor Interview (?):_____ Departmental Tour(?):_____
Audition (?):_____ Athletic Interview (?):_____
Overnight in Dorm(?):_____ Financial Aid (parents?):_____

Campus Impressions
(Rate 1 to 5; 5 being the best)

	1	2	3	4	5	Notes:
Location/Setting:	☐	☐	☐	☐	☐	
Campus Housing:	☐	☐	☐	☐	☐	
Dining:	☐	☐	☐	☐	☐	
Student Center:	☐	☐	☐	☐	☐	
Classrooms/Size:	☐	☐	☐	☐	☐	
Special Facilities:	☐	☐	☐	☐	☐	
Library/Resources:	☐	☐	☐	☐	☐	
Size/People/Friendliness:	☐	☐	☐	☐	☐	
Social Life:	☐	☐	☐	☐	☐	
Student Organizations:	☐	☐	☐	☐	☐	
Athletics:	☐	☐	☐	☐	☐	
Career Resources:	☐	☐	☐	☐	☐	
Cost/Financial Aid:	☐	☐	☐	☐	☐	

Other Information:_____
_____

Off-Campus Impressions

Cultural Information:_____
City Highlights:_____
Outdoor Activities:_____
City Transportation:_____
Student Discounts:_____

Interview Information

Interviewer's Name:_____ Thank You Note:_____
What I learned:_____

Overall Impressions

What I liked most:_____
_____

What I liked
least:_____
_____

Does this school meet my needs?_____
_____

Do I feel like I fit in? Why?_____
_____

Academic/Social Balance?_____
_____

Overall Thoughts:_____
_____

Sample Requirements Document

Colorado State University 12/1 (EA) Transcript, Scores, School Report, 1
Counselor OR 1 teacher (your choice)
Common App with Supplement 2/1 (RD) 0 recs
Honors: Separate Application due 2/1 Honors App has short essays
http://honors.colostate.edu/admissions
Scholarships: Most Scholarships-No additional application-2 scholarships have additional application https://financialaid.colostate.edu/scholarships-for-entering-non-resident-freshman/

University of Oregon 11/1 (EA) Transcript, Scores, 0 recs, School Report
Common App with Supplement 1/15 (RD)
(Choose one) Describe an experience with discrimination, whether it was fighting against discrimination or recognizing your contribution to discriminating against a person or group. What did you learn from the experience? In what ways will you bring those lessons to the University of Oregon? OR The University of Oregon values difference, and we take pride in our diverse community. Please explain how you will share your experiences, values and interests with our community. In what ways can you imagine offering your support to others? (250-500 words)
Honors: Application included as link in Common App
See choice of 3 quotes (650 words)
Scholarships: Some automatic/Must apply for some: https://financialaid.uoregon.edu/scholarships_freshmen

Syracuse University 1/1 (Reg) Transcript, Scores, Mid, School Report,
Common App with Supplement 11/15 (ED) Counselor Rec, 2 Teacher recs, CSS
Who or what influenced you to apply to Syracuse University? (Maximum: 250 words) Who is the person you dream of becoming and how do you believe Syracuse University can help you achieve this? (Maximum: 250 words)
Honors Application: You will be invited. May require extra essay.
Scholarships: Most automatic/Must apply for some: http://financialaid.syr.edu/scholarships/su/

American University 1/15 (Reg) Transcript, Scores, Mid, School Report,
Common App with Supp & Writing 11/15 (ED) Counselor Rec, 1 Teacher Rec, CSS
Why are you interested in AU? (150 words) How do you personally define an inclusive environment? What contributes to a diverse and accepting community? (400 words or fewer)
Honors Application: Separate Application due 1/15 Honors App may have separate essays
(Some Honors Programs prefer 12/15)
https://www.american.edu/admissions/freshman/special-academic-programs.cfm
Scholarships: Automatic application (except for Honors)
https://www.american.edu/financialaid/freshman-scholarships.cfm

University of New Mexico 5/1 (RD) Transcript, Scores, 0 recs
Institutional: https://admapp.unm.edu/home
Presidential Scholarship 12/1
https://scholarship.unm.edu/scholarships/resident.html   Four short essays
No application necessary for bridge and lottery scholarship
Honors College: Separate Application
https://honors.unm.edu

Sample Overall Timeline (partial)

Prior to August 11

1. Complete as much of Common App as possible.
2. Be well "on your way" with main essay (450-650 words). Possibly only 1 or 2 more drafts necessary (450-650 words).
3. Complete updated resumé.
4. Complete phone calls (and thank you email) to all admissions reps.
5. Complete as much of Coalition application as you can.

Week of Aug. 11

1. Work on University of Oregon supplement (including supplemental essay). Include link to honors application.
2. Work on University of Maryland application and supplement (Coalition).
3. Visit or make appt. to visit counselor to get any information needed for common app or coalition app. During appointment, show list of schools and ask procedure for school report, counselor recs, and transcripts. Give counselor resumé and any other necessary information.
4. Request 2 teacher recommendations. Give Resume. Get email addresses.
5. If possible, finish Common App.
6. Carry forward any assignments.

Week of Aug. 18

1. Complete University of Oregon supplement.
2. Work on University of Oregon Honors application (including essay).
3. Work on University of Maryland application and supplement (Coalition).
4. Complete FERPA agreement for all schools on Common App and request all recommendations on Common App.

Week of Aug. 25

1. Complete University of Oregon Honors application. Submit University of Oregon and UO Oregon application.
2. Complete University of Maryland application and supplement (Coalition). Submit University of Maryland.
3. Complete UNM application. Submit UNM.

Week of Sept. 1

1. Work on University of Virginia supplement.
2. Work on Boston College supplement and writing.
3. Work on Miami University supplement (including honors).
4. Request test scores to be sent to all schools.

Week of Sept. 8

1. Work on Boston College supplement and writing.
2. Work on University of Virginia supplement.
3. Work on Miami University supplement (including honors).
4. Request transcripts to be sent to all schools.

Week of Sept. 15

1. Complete Boston College supplement and writing. Submit Boston College.
2. Complete Miami University supplement (including honors). Submit Miami University Application.
3. Work on University of Wisconsin supplement.
4. Complete University of Virginia supplement. Submit University of Virginia.

Sample Homeschool Transcript

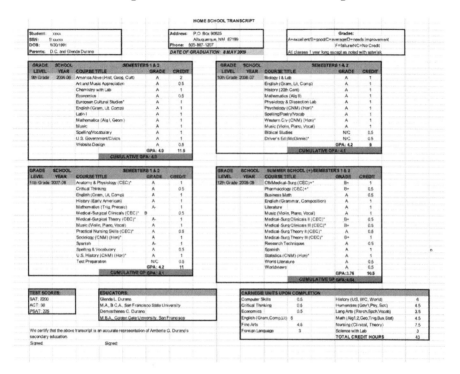

Sample Homeschool Course Descriptions

Sophomore Year 2006-2007

Algebra II/Geometry
Saxon Algebra II
The year focused on Algebra 2 and its many applications. Geometry was also included in this course.

Anatomy and Physiology/ Dissection II Lab
Fearfully and Wonderfully Made (Wile)
This in-depth course, supplemented by periodic dissection work, examined the various systems of the body and gave the student an appreciation for the incredible detail of the human anatomy.

Biblical Studies
Holy Bible, Memlock
Student memorized topical scriptures and developed personal testimony.

Biology I
Exploring Creation with Biology (Wile)
This 14-module course examined many facets of biology including cell reproduction, plant and animal classification, and genetics. Student's progress was measured using weekly tests and labs.

+Driver's Education
McGinnis School of Driving
Student completed 30 hours of classroom teaching and over 50 hours of driving practice.

English (Grammar, Composition, Literature)
Abeka Handbook of Grammar and Composition, Various Novels (see attached)
This course included grammar, composition and research techniques, and regular writing exercises. Classical literature was read and analyzed (see attached list). A major research paper was also required.

History (20th Century)
20th Century Day By Day, Our Century
By methodically examining the important events of each year of the 20th century, the student discovered the impact of recent history on the world as well as her daily life.

+Music
Violin, Piano, Vocal
Private instruction was received weekly in violin, piano, and vocal. Additionally, Amberle participated in Albuquerque Youth Orchestra and competed in various musical competitions.

+Psychology I (3 hours)
Central New Mexico Community College
This college-level course explored the basics of psychology. Due to her high grades and clear understanding of the subject matter, Amberle was invited by her professor to tutor students in Psychology as a work study for CNM.

Spelling/Vocabulary
Abeka Vocabulary and Spelling V, Wordly Wise 8, Vocabutoons II
Through utilization of several texts, the student learned the spelling and meaning of over 1000 words.

+Western Civilization II (3 hours)
Central New Mexico Community College
This was an in depth study of world events from the enlightenment to current day. Students discussed relevant issues and took chapter tests.

+These classes were not taught by parents. Professional music instructors and symphony members were utilized in teaching violin, vocal, and piano. Driver's Education was taken through a local driving school. classes at Albuquerque Central New Mexico Community College (a two-year accredited community college) were taught by full professors.

ENDNOTES

[1] https://www.cbsnews.com/news/students-attending-their-dream-colleges-at-historic-low/
[2] https://www.forbes.com/sites/camilomaldonado/2018/07/24/price-of-college-increasing-almost-8-times-faster-than-wages/#5770d14366c1
[3] https://research.collegeboard.org/trends/college-pricing/figures-tables/average-published-charges-2018-19-and-2019-20
[4] https://www.vocativ.com/usa/education-usa/college-admissions-accepted-first-choice/index.html
[5] https://www.cnbc.com/2019/04/24/tuition-at-public-universities-is-10230-a-year-on-average.html
[6] https://www.washingtonpost.com/business/get-real-on-scholarships/ 2011/03/08/